L

Ple

V 2011

L

THE LIGHTNING BOYS

THE
LIGHTNING BOYS

True Tales From Pilots Of
The English Electric Lightning

RICHARD PIKE

Grub Street • London

Published by
Grub Street
4 Rainham Close
London
SW11 6SS

Copyright © Grub Street 2011
Copyright text © Richard Pike 2011

British Library Cataloguing in Publication Data
Pike, Richard.
The Lightning boys : true tales from pilots of the English
Electric Lightning.
1. Lightning (Fighter plane)—Anecdotes. 2. Air pilots,
Military—Anecdotes.
I. Title
623.7'464'0922-dc22

ISBN-13: 9781908117151

Cover design by Sarah Driver based on the painting 'Reheat Rotation' by
Chris Stone
Edited by Sophie Campbell
Formatted by Sarah Driver

Printed and bound by MPG Ltd, Bodmin, Cornwall

Grub Street Publishing only uses
FSC (Forest Stewardship Council) paper for its books.

CONTENTS

ACKNOWLEDGEMENTS

Many of those involved with Lightning operations, commonly known as WIWOLs (When I Was On Lightnings), have maintained a strong bond since the aircraft was decommissioned in 1988. A website run by Ed Durham, a former CO of a Lightning squadron, is evidence of this. *The Lightning Boys* was greatly facilitated by Ed's encouragement and co-operation, despite ill-health, and by his wide network of contacts within the Lightning world.

The painting 'Reheat Rotation' by Chris Stone, reproduced in this book with his kind permission, is currently displayed in the Royal Air Force Club, Piccadilly, London.

The author and publisher would like to thank all those who contributed photographs and pictures; including all the Lightning pilots who provided photographs of themselves, with special thanks to Ed Durham, Simon Watson, Roger Colebrook, Graham Perry, John Hall, Alan White and Chris Stone.

DEDICATION

To those from factory floor to admin desk to engineering support whose activities gave Lightning pilots so much excitement.

Chapter 1

FIERY BAPTISM

ROGER COLEBROOK'S FLAMING FIRST FLIGHT

Pilot Officer Roger Colebrook, Hunter OCU 1966.

He gave me a sideways glance but he said nothing at first. We stood by the line hut and I was conscious of his inscrutable expression, his serious, searching eyes. Later these would prove invaluable attributes, no doubt, for this future air chief marshal and chief of the air staff, but this was 1966 – Monday 24th October, to be precise – and as my flying instructor at the time, he had to make a crucial decision. The slightly-built Flight Lieutenant M J Graydon glanced at me again. He shifted uncomfortably from foot to foot. He coughed dryly. "The next exercise in the syllabus," he said at last, "is to do exactly what we've just done, only this time on your own." He hesitated. "Do you think you're up to it?"

I paused then said: "Yes." Perhaps I sounded a little flat. Maybe I should have felt a little more excited. This, after all, would be my first solo flight in a Lightning aircraft, surely every pilot's dream. In truth, though, I saw it as no particular big deal, just another hurdle to be

7

cleared in the seemingly endless air force training machine.

My instructor nodded. "Very well," he said. "The engineers will sort out which aircraft you'll take. It may well be that one..." he waved towards Lightning T4 XM 968, a dual-control machine parked near XM973, the T4 Lightning we had just flown together, "then you can get going." With its side-by-side dual control arrangement, the Lightning T4's cockpit layout was different from the single-seat Lightning F1A which we would fly later in the course. Prudence dictated that for our first solo flight we rookie students should stick to a familiar cockpit layout.

"OK," I said.

At this, we stepped inside the engineering line hut, signed the technical log, briefed the engineers, and headed towards the Lightning pilots' crewroom. "Coffee?" I asked my instructor.

"Yes please – standard NATO." This meant a mug of white coffee with two generous teaspoons of sugar applied.

A mood of reflection struck me as I dealt with the makings. I was, after all, just a young lad, barely twenty years of age. I only wished that I could have told my parents and my brother this news about my first solo flight on Lightnings. How marvellous if they could have felt proud of me, if they could have shared the moment. But it wouldn't have worked; I could not have told them. It would only have caused upset. My father, as a flight sergeant photographer in the RAF when he retired in 1957, had seemed to resent the fact that I had joined the service as an officer. Not once had he asked me what I did, or what type of aircraft I flew, or about my progress. My mother, God bless her, had no inkling what purpose I served. I had never even told them, for instance, that I had won the Glen Trophy at 3 Flying Training School, a prize awarded to the best overall pilot. That would have been deemed boastful. My brother, four-and-a-half years my senior, was an agricultural engineer and my mother had always blamed his poor performance on the large number of postings that went with service life.

For my own part, I had joined the service for a variety of reasons. I wanted to fly, I wanted to be a fighter pilot, and I liked the idea of a job that involved protecting the country and its way of life. As my training had progressed, I had been impressed by the way the service seemed to offer learning and experience above and beyond pure professional expertise. There was a culture of excellence; meritorious achievement counted above accident of birth. Few cared whether someone had been born into a respectable residence within easy contact of London, or brought up within the grimmer, tighter north, the backstreets of Leeds or Newcastle for instance, with lesser access to style and wealth. Social deference was virtually nonexistent; deference to hierarchical military rank ruled. Beyond this rigid rank-consciousness, service life strived to gloss over the niceties of upper working class, lower middle class, upper this, lower that, middle the other, the subtle variations of social location. *Per ardua ad astra* was expected and exemplified from the top: the dreary slide of standards of some air marshals-to-be; the sordid ambition (that master-passion which seemed to take the place of honour), even downright incompetence and consequent deflation of ego of an individual sacked, for example, for overzealous home improvement using public funds, or one whose even more zealous extra-marital exposure by the press forced the marshal of the RAF to resign...all of that lay in the future. Most Lightning pilots rose above such machinations; maybe a sense of sheer survival made this necessary.

To date I had flown six dual-control flights with my instructor, and a total of just over four flying hours on the Lightning – not much for such a powerful, awesome machine. My grand total of flying hours, 325, was significant compared to the poor souls of an earlier generation, the Spitfire and Hurricane pilots of a mere quarter century ago, but was still less than earth-shattering. The Lightning seemed such an enormous beast. After some of the other types I had flown in training, especially the tiny Folland Gnat, the preflight walk-around checks, for one thing, could seem quite intimidating. Remarkably, the Lightning was roughly the same weight as some of the later marks of Wellington bomber used by Bomber Command in the Second World War. Unlike the massive bomb loads of the Wellington, however, an armed Lightning would carry just two missiles – and rather puny ones at that, some would say. There was the Firestreak missile, otherwise known as 'Firewood', or the supposedly more advanced Red Top (dubbed 'Red Flop' by the pilots).

I handed my instructor a mug of steaming coffee. "As ordered, one standard NATO..." He nodded thanks then gestured towards a quiet corner of the crewroom where he would debrief me on the recent flight, and brief me on the next.

"Remember," he said, "to plan and to think well ahead...stay on top of things and don't allow the machine to race ahead of your mental processes. When you've finished the high level work, return to Coltishall airfield for a few practise circuits. Watch your airspeed on finals and concentrate on the runway perspective. I want you to carry out a couple of approaches and overshoots before your final landing..." Further pearls of wisdom ensued then, with the briefing complete, we had to wait for word from the engineers. I offered to make my instructor another mug of coffee but he declined.

As we waited, I glanced around the crewroom. One or two individuals sat about, some who boned up on Lightning pilots' notes, one man who observed activity outside, another who studied a newspaper. This was unusual; the packed course syllabus normally precluded time for newspaper reading. However, last Friday's disaster at Aberfan was on all of our minds and a subject of sad discussion.

Shocked by Aberfan, the good folk of the flower-power 1960s had other issues too. Scepticism was growing. There was market research, there were leather jackets. Trendy-lefty speak was catching on. New ideas, new freedoms sprang up. Serious, severe sociologists from the University of Essex demanded to be heard. Young men grew stubbly beards (deemed unmilitary and inappropriate for steely fighter pilots). Young women wore mini-skirts. People worried about detergents, black Americans, the Beatles, Rhodesia, Vietnam, abortion, Coronation Street.

For those of us in the military, the Cold War was an all-consuming focus. The Lightning force, backed by a system of ground-based missiles, was charged with the defence of our island skies. The general idea was to scramble at lightning speed, zoom up to the required altitude, then with a combination of ground radar directions and our own on-board radar, intercept and shoot down the Soviet hordes. We would let them have it with a bit of Firewood – a couple of Red Flops if they were lucky – before we dashed back to base to rearm, refuel, and hurtle off again to repeat the process.

There were, unfortunately, flaws within this mega-strategy. For one thing, the Soviet hordes, when they arrived, were likely to outnumber us by a ratio of approximately thirty to one. Other than the implausible scenario that the Soviets would play ball, do the decent thing, be thoroughly British and orbit patiently while we rearmed and refuelled, we faced something of a David and Goliath struggle. I sometimes speculated on the reaction of Dowding, leader of Fighter Command in the Battle of Britain, to this plan. Perhaps he would have said nothing. Perhaps his cold, hard stare accompanied by the lifting of one eyebrow would have sufficed.

"Roger – you're on..." At last we received the waited call from the engineers. My mouth felt dry. I swallowed hard. I experienced an odd mixture of sentiments, as if I was a condemned man but one who was anxious to proceed anyway. In my mind I hastily recapped my flying instructor's briefing. He looked at me and the grave, grey expression was characteristic as he said: "I'm sure everything will be OK. In case of trouble I'll be in the air traffic control tower to follow your progress. Don't worry; this is normal routine – standard practice for first solo flights on the Lightning."

As I walked to the engineering line hut, I carried my white flying helmet, otherwise known as a bone dome, in one hand. The racket of Lightning aircraft engine noise was pervasive and I had to remain alert to the dangers of approaching aircraft and vehicles. When inside the line hut, I gave a friendly nod to the line chief. "All ready for you, sir," he said, "good kite this one." The elderly chiefie breathed confidentially into my ear: "Shouldn't give you no bother." He winked. In the background, a battered radio set played music from The Supremes latest hit album. I put my bone dome on the table, checked the aircraft log, scrawled a signature, and glanced at the chiefie as if for further encouragement. This time, though, he just stared at me blankly. I managed a grin, picked up my bone dome, and stepped outside before I headed for Her Majesty's aircraft, Lightning T4 XM968.

My walk-around check was observed by an allocated ground crewman. He had placed a fire extinguisher to one side of the aircraft from where he would supervise the start-up procedure. He remained there, arms folded, as if bored and cold. I was determined, though, not to be rushed. Firstly I stood at the front of the aircraft and looked upwards to

XM968 flown by Roger Colebrook.
Reproduced with thanks to Airlife Publishing

verify that the engine intake was clear. I checked the extended pitot-static tube to ensure that the protective cover had been removed. I inspected the radar dome in the centre of the engine air intake. When switched on once airborne, the ingenious radar within its dome would whizz from side to side, up and down, like some demented leprechaun, and would be the cause of much anguish to come. At this stage in the course, though, my job was to concentrate on how to handle the aircraft itself.

Now I moved back to inspect the starboard side of the aircraft, including the undercarriage mechanism and wheels. The Lightning's undercarriage was a particular science. The tyres, thin enough to fit into the aircraft's slender wings, yet rugged enough to cope with the high take-off and landing speeds, were specially designed and manufactured. They were also, so we were told, very expensive. With luck, a tyre might last up to ten landings, however a strong cross-wind could wreck a tyre in just one flight. At the time, however, such thoughts were far from my mind. I bent low to inspect the starboard tyre and associated brake assembly before I walked to the rear of the aircraft. Once there, I stared up into the black wilderness of the aircraft's twin jet pipes set one above the other. My sense of awe was intense. What power, what heat, what sheer brute force would be thrust through those complex pipes! Lastly, I checked the port side of the aircraft before I stepped up the boarding ladder hooked onto the cockpit side, and clambered aboard. The ground crewman assisted as I strapped-in to the left-hand seat. He confirmed that the ejection seat safety pins were removed, then stepped down and detached the boarding ladder before he returned to his position by the fire extinguisher.

The pre-start procedure was second nature to me by that stage. As a keen student, I had spent hours in the classroom, in the flight simulator and in the cockpit of a hangar-bound aircraft in order to learn the cockpit drills. I glanced across at the adjacent empty seat secured by a safety apron, then went through the well-rehearsed cockpit drills...*check position of the twin throttles, flight instruments set, engine instruments okay, fuel contents full, oxygen sufficient*... My mind was entirely focused on the task in hand and soon I was ready to start the first engine. I raised one finger to the ground crewman, made a circling motion to indicate engine start, and received a thumbs-up sign. I looked inside the cockpit again, located the engine start buttons, and pressed the relevant one. A shrill *wheeee* followed by a sudden crashing noise indicated commencement of the first engine's start cycle. I checked the engine instruments, confirmed that all looked in order, made another circling sign to the ground crewman, and repeated the start procedure for the other engine.

With both engines happily turning and burning, I was ready to taxi out for take-off. I pressed the radio transmit button and spoke with Coltishall air traffic control. The controller's voice sounded unflustered and comforting as he replied: "968...clear to taxi for runway..." After a last thumbs-up from the ground crewman to indicate wheel chocks removed, I released the parking brake and allowed the machine to ease forward. By regular squeezes on the brake handle by the control stick I limited the aircraft's speed to a fast walking pace. I kicked the rudder pedals left or right to obtain directional control by means of differential braking, and before long I was on the main taxiway headed for the day's runway-in-use, as determined by the wind direction.

"968...clear for take-off..." the local controller, a distant figure behind long panes of glass in the Coltishall air traffic control tower, now allowed me to move directly onto the runway. As I progressed towards the take-off point, he appeared to observe proceedings through binoculars. There was no time to bother about this, however, as I turned the Lightning onto the runway, made a final check of cockpit instruments, and quickly recapped in my mind the take-off procedure. For this flight, I had been briefed to use 'cold power', which meant no reheat (or afterburner as the Americans would say). I would have to be careful, therefore, not to push the throttles through a friction gate to the 'reheat' section.

When lined-up on the runway, I brought the machine to a halt – unlike the procedure for a 'scramble' take-off – and visually checked that the runway and climb-out area were unobstructed. All looked clear. I was ready to go. The moment had come.

Slowly but firmly I advanced both throttles to the 'full cold power' position and released the brakes. At once the machine sprang forward and I felt a kick in my back. Apart from occasional glances at the airspeed indicator, I concentrated on looking outside the cockpit. My peripheral vision picked up a blur to each side as the Lightning accelerated. With my left hand I ensured the twin throttles were held fully forward in the correct position; with my right hand I made minor flight control inputs to counter crosswind effect. In what felt like no time, the airspeed indicator was passing 100 knots...110 knots...120 knots...the acceleration continued. At just the right moment I eased back on the control stick to raise the nose-wheel off the ground, the main wheels followed and suddenly I was airborne.

Now I had to act fast; the Lightning did not hang about, even in cold power. The altimeter began to wind up as I gained height and swiftly I raised the undercarriage as part of the after-take-off checks. There was so much to remember...*keep a good lookout...maintain a mental plot of position...monitor the flight instruments...constantly check fuel contents...* Amongst other bones of contention, the Lightning was notorious for its lack of available fuel. We had been told as an example that if reheat was engaged at low level and the machine flown in a continuous tight turn, the entire fuel load could be consumed in about ten minutes. This instance may have sounded a little extreme, nonetheless the average sortie length for some marks of Lightning was no more than around forty minutes.

As I gained height, and as the distinctive outline of the Norfolk coast and The Wash beyond formed a real-life map ahead, I continued to maintain a good visual lookout. Numerous Norfolk villages showed up to the side and in front, but I had to twist my head back in order to glimpse the city of Norwich. This, however, was good practice. From square one, we budding fighter pilots had been taught the need to pay heed to the area behind us. Perhaps a hangover from Battle of Britain days when the 'Hun in the sun' and 'watch your six o'clock' were key watchwords to survival, the principles remained good ones. They were certainly pointed out regularly by our instructors. Good lookout may have been the emphasis, nevertheless aircraft systems could not be ignored. I darted a glance inside my cockpit for an expeditious look around the 'office'. I quickly checked instruments, airspeed at 450 knots, height approaching 6,000 feet, fuel contents, warning panels, and then I looked outside again. For my mental processes to stay ahead of the aircraft, my mind was centred entirely on the world within and surrounding my cockpit, on the immediate task in hand. I had no time to think about the goings-on of lives below, of the individuals who may have looked up as the noisy Lightning roared overhead, of the folk in their cars, in their gardens, in the houses that backed onto them...

CLANG...CLANG...CLANG... my concentration was interrupted by an electronically generated warning bell in my bone dome earpieces. I glanced again inside the cockpit. A fire warning light had blinked on; a fire in number one engine was indicated. At once, I pulled back the number one engine throttle and closed down the engine. This caused angry swarms of further warning lights to appear. I checked the engine's jet pipe temperature gauge, carried out drills, and pressed the affected engine's fire extinguisher button. The red 'FIRE 1' warning light, however, continued to glow brightly. Now I put out an emergency radio call – "PAN...PAN...PAN" – and simultaneously turned left to head back towards Coltishall. "You're clear direct to the airfield..." The controller's voice was still unflustered and I thought my instructor's voice could be heard in the background.

With the immediate drills completed, I recapped my actions so far. I appreciated, at that second, the benefit of the flight simulator exercises. My actions and reactions up to this stage had been pretty much automatic. Now, though, there were further considerations, especially as the FIRE 1 warning light remained on. I prompted myself to 'think fuel'. Directly beneath the number one engine was a fuel ventral tank which might go 'bang' if the engine fire spread. I should jettison the ventral tank without delay. This I did, and rechecked the FIRE 1 light which, to my considerable relief, now went out.

At this point, I eased back the number two engine throttle to expedite my descent. I kept a careful eye on this engine for signs of damage which might have been caused by the fire in number one. All indications, though, remained normal. The day was cloudless and as Coltishall airfield came into sight, I aimed for a position on the downwind leg of the aerodrome circuit at a height of 1,000 feet. "You have priority," said the air traffic controller, "you're clear direct to the downwind leg."

"Understood," I said. I tried to judge my arrival in the circuit so as to use minimum power; I was becoming concerned by the aircraft's low fuel state. The ventral tank fuel was lost when I jettisoned the tank, even so the fuel reading seemed abnormally low. At the appropriate point I selected the undercarriage down as part of the pre-landing checks. During these checks, I saw that the fuel contents were now dangerously low. Later, my instructor would tell me that he had seen vapour streaming from the underside of the aircraft but that he hadn't wished to say anything for fear of causing alarm and despondency. He had assumed the vapour to be smoke from the engine fire, but in fact the cause was a fuel leak; the ventral tank seal had been damaged when I jettisoned the tank and I was rapidly losing internal fuel.

As I turned towards the airfield and called: "968 on finals," another quick check of the fuel gauges revealed just 400lbs; at the end of a normal sortie of forty or so minutes they should have indicated around 1,600lbs but I had been airborne for less than ten minutes. My landing would need to be a good one; there would be no second chance. I remembered my instructor's advice about runway perspective and I tried to concentrate on making this the best of my few Lightning landings to date. There was a thump as the expensive tyres made contact with the runway, after which I activated the tail chute. The chute, although slower than normal, deployed successfully. Now I applied the brakes and aimed to taxi clear of the runway to where fire crews awaited. As the Lightning rolled to a halt I became aware of my tight grip on the brake lever. "For God's sake relax," I told myself.

"Nice flight, sir?"A fireman grinned and tried to act jauntily as he placed a ladder by the side of the cockpit. He inserted the ejection seat safety pins then helped me to climb down. When my feet touched *terra firma* I felt a prompt sense of relief. My flight had not ended with a 'Martin Baker let-down' – an enforced use of the Martin Baker ejection seat. I had not ended up dangling ignominiously on the end of a parachute. The flight had lasted fewer than ten minutes, but at least I had brought the machine back in one piece. I had made mistakes, no doubt, and these would be pointed out by my instructor, but overall I felt quite pleased with my performance.

My instructor waited in the crewroom as the fire crews drove me there. "Well, well," he said when I walked in. "That was a good learning exercise, Roger." I admired his positive spin on events. I busied myself with making yet more mugs of standard NATO coffees, and as I did so, became aware that several instructors were coming up to me to engage in rather forced conversation. This was highly unorthodox. Humble students did not normally qualify for much in the way of general conversation, polite or otherwise. Not until later did I realise that the staff were trying to decide whether my state of mind allowed another attempt at 'first' solo or whether I needed a further confidence-boosting dual flight. At length, my instructor said that another Lightning T4 was being prepared and that I should be on my way again soon. Evidently I had been declared officially sane.

The second of my attempts at first solo went smoothly enough, except that as I hurtled down the runway during take-off, the warning bell sounded once more. 'Good God,' I thought. 'Not again, and so soon…' Instinctively, I closed the throttles in anticipation of another fire. However a quick glance at the warning panel revealed not a fire but a minor oxygen problem. The oxygen supply to the instructor's side had, quite correctly, been disconnected. A slow loss of pressure had triggered the alarm. Cursing myself for a fool, I pushed the throttles forward again and continued the take-off.

Following the subsequent forty minutes of flight, my instructor carried out a thorough debrief. This ended with something along the lines of: "I reckon we've earned ourselves a beer or two." I did not disagree with this suggestion and we arranged to meet up in the officers' mess bar. I decided, though, there was something that should be done first.

I left the crewroom and walked up to the hangar where Lightning T4 XM968 was securely ensconced. The recalcitrant aircraft, now pathetic and forlorn-looking, had been placed on special jacks. Jet pipes had been removed, panels opened, wires were sticking out. I would learn later that the cockpit warning had been no false alarm; the fire had been real enough. Engineers crawled about the machine, examined this and that, peered here and there, and scratched their heads in perplexity. The signs of fire or flames were absent now, the recent drama had become history, but for me the memory persisted. I had received a shock, but fire in the air was not so unusual in a Lightning. I had been lucky; I had been able to fly back to base. This would not be the case for others. As I gazed at the machine and the surrounding activity, I thought back to just a few years ago when I was a mere lad in his early teenage years. I had been intrigued by the RAF's announcement in July 1960 that the new Lightning twin-engined, single-seat fighter would enter service with 74 Squadron at Coltishall. I had been interested in the aircraft, read up details, wondered at the skill and courage of the pilots, the *crème de la crème*. I had admired all of this, nonetheless my main ambition had been to fly ground-attack aircraft, such as the Hawker Hunter. At the Advanced Flying Training School at Valley, Anglesey, I had been rather disappointed when told I was to be posted onto Lightnings. However, my chief objective in life had been achieved. I had been selected to become a fighter pilot...

I continued to stare at XM968. My thoughts, as involved as the network of wires, pipes, panels exhibited as engineers delved deeper into the machine's innards, seemed in turmoil. I felt at once bothered and buoyant, clear and confused. I pondered how the mulish mentality created by one serious incident had almost caused another. This day I had learnt much, but I still had much to learn. I must have stood there for quite a long time.

Chapter 2

GORILLA
TACTICS

Flight Lieutenant Bill Wratten,
19 Squadron, RAF Gütersloh 1967.
At the time Bill was the RAF Germany
Lightning display pilot, the squadron QFI
and the RAF Germany Command IRE.

BILL WRATTEN'S
AEROBATIC DAYS

It all began in February 1967. I was a member of 19 (Fighter) Squadron and my commanding officer, Wing Commander Brian Cox, had agreed to let me develop an aerobatic sequence. I had to prove to him that I was competent to display the Lightning at low level at public events. Exciting stuff! I was eager to anticipate the chance for some great flying and I was keen to show off the most marvellous aircraft ever to grace the skies. Looking back, my motives, I'm sure, were honourable; personal ego was low on the list. At least, I think it was. I was equally sure that I had to be honest with myself if the challenge proved beyond me. My boss, though, was encouraging and he undertook to witness every rehearsal if and when I was cleared to display at low level over the airfield. He would not hesitate to let me know if the display looked either pedestrian or suicidal. I would be very much on trial.

So the hard work commenced. I was cleared to practise at progressively lower heights – 5,000 feet, then 3,000 feet, 1,500 feet, 1,000 feet – all of which went fairly well. The sequence was adjusted to what I felt was a fair compromise between maximum performance and good presentation. I attempted to ensure that the exit speed from one manoeuvre matched the entry speed of the next. I aimed for a minimum time interval between each manoeuvre so there was no waiting by spectators. I tried to make the performance riveting for the layman (noise and speed) and acceptable to fellow Lightning pilots (accuracy, consistency, high difficulty index). My boss seemed content with progress thus far and I felt as confident as I thought I should be at that stage. But the magical milestone remained: clearance for the first rehearsal with loops down to 500 feet over the airfield, and rolls, slow rolls, Derry turns down to 250 feet.

This milestone was reached in May 1967. I received the message that I had been granted the necessary clearance and my first practice at these heights would be on 8th May 1967 in Lightning Mark 2 XN791.

By that stage, my sequence was timed to last about seven-and-a-half minutes from the slow speed entry to the high speed departure. I had felt reasonably happy with the practices at 1,000 feet but now, at these new low altitudes, I found myself in another world. I could barely take in what was happening around me. The time passed in a blur of disbelief. I could not begin to understand why I was never where I should have been over the airfield; my airspeed was all over the shop; the loops were ragged; the rolls were hurried and rough as old boots; my hyperventilation defied the laws of medical science. I breathed so rapidly that I should have lapsed into unconsciousness. Eventually I landed, soaking wet with perspiration, and when I taxied-in I felt thoroughly depressed and deflated. I only hoped that none of my colleagues had been watching. I anticipated a facial expression from the boss that would advise me to stick to my job as the squadron QFI (qualified flying instructor).

The boss, though, remained reasonably upbeat. He said that it wasn't so bad for a first go. He then went on to describe how I had probably felt, how I had seen things happen ten times faster than expected and that I never felt properly positioned or prepared for the next event. In other words, I was just not quite fully in charge of my aeroplane.

The accuracy of these comments surprised me very considerably, to say the least, and from that moment I listened avidly to his every word during debriefs. I found he had a disarming knack of being critical without causing me to feel demoralised. On the contrary, I learnt quickly to anticipate what he would say about every single manoeuvre. I found his talent for visualising from the ground what I was doing in the cockpit more than encouraging. He managed to keep me on the right side of that precarious line that separates despair from enthusiasm. Even after a particularly difficult rehearsal, when the wind would blow me towards the display line to where my eventual spectators would be standing (the dreaded 'on-crowd' wind), and when individual manoeuvre accuracy had to suffer to ensure correct positioning (this being the priority – there is no point in impeccable flying if no-one can see it) – even then his professional, analytical advice would help me to improve next time.

So it was that the many practices eventually began to bear fruit. At length, I was formally cleared for public display flying as RAF Germany's Lightning display pilot for 1967. I felt tickled pink! The hard work, the copious debriefs, the many lessons learnt, all added a new and unforeseen dimension to my love of flying – something I have treasured ever since. I developed a new-found confidence; I felt better able to cope with the unexpected. To enter cloud at the top of a loop, for example, no longer caused me concern; I learnt to adjust the aircraft's positioning for the longest of display lines (Brussels International Airport) and the shortest (Werl Flying Club, Germany). I became adept at coping with 'on-crowd' winds and the requisite adjustments to the timing of reheat selection; I could start my sequence over an airfield's display line whatever the direction of the wind, or whatever the position of the holding pattern away from the airfield. In short, knowledge and confidence grew together, the former leading to the latter as in any profession.

That is not to claim that I made no mistakes. None, fortunately, were in any way disastrous, but I suffered oversights no less than any pilot. For the main it was allowing myself to be rushed in a way that interfered with my disciplined habits and good practices that had been drilled into place during rigorous rehearsals. One of the more serious of these occurred when I agreed, perhaps with a little too much self-assurance, to have my display slot brought forward so that my time from the flight line to take-off was severely reduced. My subsequent display was flown in the middle of one of the hottest and most humid days that the North German Plain could generate, and on landing I felt so unwell that I was tempted to request an ambulance to meet me. Thank goodness I didn't for when I carried out the shut-down checks I discovered that the whole sortie had been flown without cockpit pressurisation. I had failed to carry out my pre-start checks properly and without the cockpit pressurisation there was no cockpit cooling. In effect, I had displayed the Lightning while sitting in a Turkish bath. What an admission to have to make!

There were lighter sides too. To this day I cannot resist a smile when I think back to a comical incident on another hot summer's day when my aircraft was parked alongside those of the illustrious Red Arrows display team. I chatted and joked with members of the team, at that time regarded as the best formation aerobatic team in the world with members like Henry Prince, Roy Booth, Ernie Jones and their legendary leader, Ray Hanna. I was especially glad to exchange ideas with Ernie Jones who had been Fighter Command's Lightning display pilot when my squadron, 19 Squadron, was based at Leconfield just before we, together with 92 Squadron, moved to RAF Germany. I had particular admiration for him, his reputation for consistency and accuracy was held in high regard, and I was eager to learn what he thought of my efforts. So we talked for a while before the heat overtook us all and we simply lounged about, stripped down to our underpants as we were positioned on the far side of the airfield with the closest civilisation a couple of miles away.

A half hour or so into this state of torpor one of the Red Arrows team members, Henry Prince, got to his feet, moved a few yards away from the rest of us and proceeded to relieve himself. This was considered perfectly reasonable as the nearest lavatory was inaccessible and no-one was about to be offended by such an act of necessity. Moreover, the rest of the team appeared to ignore him completely. Or so I thought. I soon began to realise, however, that the apparent disinterest was anything but because, as soon as poor Henry had reached his point-of-no-return, so to speak, out came a veritable multitude of cameras, including cine cameras, to place on record the biological needs of one of the Red Arrows synchro pair pilots thus proving that he was human after all.

This was innocent enough stuff but it captured the spontaneity, camaraderie and sense of humour of those nine flying aces (eight, perhaps, as the whole incident was above the dignity of their leader) and demonstrated a team at the height of its confidence, a team whose personalities delighted

in each others' company. Despite the challenge of formation display aerobatics, especially in the tense period immediately before a display when
there is little else to do but dwell on the essential need for a safe but compelling performance, they still found time for a bit of fun. At least, that
was the way I saw things.

It was towards the end of my year's display season, when I least expected it, that I would learn a less-than-amusing lesson. This would turn
out to be a salutary experience which would have implications much later
in my service career. The personal worries about making the grade I had
felt at the start of the display season had been conquered and I had reached
the stage where I was thoroughly enjoying the display circuit. I had been
fortunate: nothing particularly abnormal or untoward had occurred and I
had managed to carry out the sequences pretty much to my complete satisfaction. Positioning and manoeuvre accuracy had been honed to a high
standard and by then I was sure that I was concentrating on the essentials.
I felt that I knew exactly when to engage or disengage reheat, and precisely
how much 'g' to pull at every stage to match the speed and height needed
for accurate positioning over the ground. Moreover, the routine had become instinctive and as far removed from the exhausting and hurried efforts of those early days as it was possible to be. While things did not
exactly happen in slow motion, I found there was time to get it right from
the outset, time to ensure my mental processes were ahead of the aircraft
no matter what the prevailing wind, cloud and visibility. This was a highly
satisfactory state of mind in which to conduct one of the most demanding
of flying disciplines.

If my new-found confidence was in danger of drifting towards over-
confidence, if my thoughts of self-satisfaction about how, for one thing,
the hyperventilation of the early days really had become a thing of the
past, then it was the Lightning's warning system that brought me rapidly
round to reality. One day, in the middle of a display, the cockpit lights, accompanied by a clanging sound in my headset earpieces, imperiously, tiresomely, announced an aircraft emergency.

At once, I looked down to check the aircraft SWP (standard warning
panel). I could hardly believe my eyes. I felt a surge of astonishment, almost panic, rise within me. The panel's cover was missing: instead of clear
information about the nature of the emergency, I saw a series of bare bulbs
instead. Unless – and PDQ – I could figure out from memory the aircraft
system represented by each bulb, especially the one that now glowed omi-

nously, the information on the warning panel was meaningless.

Fortunately, as the squadron QFI part of my job was to test the other pilots on their knowledge of the aircraft's cockpit and other systems. By a process of cross-checking and counting down the panel's bulbs I concluded that an engine fire warning had been triggered. Immediately, I carried out the appropriate drill, put out an emergency radio call, and received clearance from air traffic control for a priority landing. The landing was without incident and I managed to taxi the Lightning clear of the runway. I then handed the aircraft over to engineers who would investigate the fire warning as well as carry out a search for the missing panel cover.

When one of the smaller engineers lowered himself head-first into the cockpit, he soon found the missing item. The cover was lying in the bottom of the cockpit not, as might have been expected, jammed into any awkward corner but merely lying loose. This bothered me. It bothered me a great deal. How on earth could I have flown a low-level aerobatic display, pulled all manner of positive 'g', pushed negative 'g' until my eyes bulged out, exposed the airframe and everything within it to merciless violence without noticing that a large piece of solid metal was rattling around in front of my very eyes? The potential danger weighed heavily on my mind, and that of my boss's too. I told him simply, and truthfully, that I just hadn't seen it. The matter was as straightforward and as unsatisfactory as that. I am sure that it was only the good rapport that had developed between us which allowed him to accept this. I was off the hook but the worry persisted, and indeed continued for a long time. If I had missed that, what else could I miss? Was there something wrong with my powers of observation, something sinister, perhaps, something that my black imagination was attempting to conjure up?

The solution came to me later, years later in fact, and completely by chance. I happened to see a video clip – seen, no doubt, by millions of others too – which was designed to reveal the problem of intense concentration on a specific task at the expense of all else. A test, in other words, to highlight the dangers of tunnel vision. In the test, an observer was asked to count how many times a large ball was bounced between two people in a gathering of some half-dozen others who moved around the two ball bouncers. The test was not difficult and few got it wrong. When the pertinent question was asked – "did you notice anything unusual going on as you counted the number of ball bounces?" – almost everyone replied that they had not. The video clip was then played again and, much to the observers' astonishment and embarrassment, they would see a man dressed as a gorilla suddenly appear and start to dance about amongst the ball bouncers. Such was the concentration on counting the number of ball bounces that, first time around, the observers had failed to spot the gorilla. When I applied this principle to my incident with the loose warning panel cover, all became promptly, and painfully clear.

I never forgot the implications of this episode and, as it happened, there were ramifications at a much later stage in my service career *(from 1994 to 1997, Air Chief Marshal Sir William J Wratten GBE CB AFC was air officer commander-in-chief, RAF Strike Command – Editor)*. There was one case, for example, which was referred to me and which concerned a tragic incident involving a first-tour Jaguar pilot on his operational conversion course, then based at Lossiemouth on the Moray Firth in Scotland. This pilot had not been doing too well on his course so was under greater pressure than would have been the case for a more gifted individual. One day he was programmed to fly as number four in his first four-ship formation exercise. The formation lined up for take-off and, as number four, the young man in question was the last to launch. He released the aircraft brakes, commenced the take-off run but regretfully he failed to engage reheat. The Jaguar, which does not perform well in cold power on take-off, consequently failed to clear the crash barrier at the far end of the runway. The pilot was killed.

The subsequent board of inquiry concluded that by his failure to select reheat, the pilot had been negligent. According to the service's definition of negligence, he had done something a reasonable pilot would not have done. Both the station commander and the air officer commanding agreed with the board of inquiry's findings, but I did not. I went back to my warning panel experience in the Lightning, and the sudden, sobering revelation when I had watched the gorilla video. Even though I was a young man at the time, I was an experienced combat-ready pilot, a qualified flying instructor, an instrument rating examiner, and a fully-cleared display pilot. Despite all of these qualifications, I was hypnotised by the demands of total concentration, I had tunnel vision if you like, and I had missed the patently obvious. How much more likely might it have been for the Jaguar student – already stretched to the limits of his ability, conscious of the demanding sortie ahead, eager to do well, anxious to join up quickly with his three colleagues ahead – to have overlooked one of the most basic but crucial demands of all as he started his take-off run?

I seldom found the need to disagree with any of my station commanders or air-officers-commanding, but on this occasion I did. I amended the
board of inquiry's findings to one of 'error of judgement', which meant in
effect that the young pilot had done his best but that all of the concurrent
demands of the moment had, for him, simply become too many.

The instance of some thirty years previously and my subsequent comprehension through watching the gorilla video had exerted a powerful influence on me. An influence, indeed, that was far greater than I would ever
have believed possible at the time.

Chapter 3

TOUCH
AND GO

*ROSS PAYNE
TRIES TO LAND*

Binbrook, an airfield in Lincolnshire, is notorious for few things apart from a position of remoteness and a reputation amongst pilots for fickle winds. It was early on a Monday morning on 12th March 1979 when I arrived at work to discover that the wind was up to its usual unhelpful tricks – tiresomely gusty and from an inconvenient direction directly across the runway. Furthermore, the wind was forecast to increase in strength as the morning progressed. I had come in specially because, in my capacity as a Lightning aerobatic display pilot, I wanted to carry out a rehearsal before the day's normal flying programme commenced. I was an instructor on the Lightning Training Flight and, following the aerobatic practice, I had a busy schedule planned.

A quick check of the weather charts and a conversation with the forecaster suggested that, despite the difficult winds, it should still be possible for me to conduct my aerobatic sequence. However I needed to hurry as there was a danger that, once the wind strength began to increase, stipulated flying limits might be reached. My flight was therefore authorised and soon I was hastening to the line hut to check the technical log of my allocated machine, and from there I walked quickly to the aircraft itself. Soon I had checked the outside of the aircraft and was strapping-in to the single-seat Lightning Mark 3. Slickly, I went through the pre-start checks, fired-up both engines, and obtained clearance from air traffic control to taxi out for take-off.

The take-off went according to plan, as did the initial part of my aerobatic sequence. This sequence included an inverted run at 500 feet above the runway, and it was at the end of the run, with my eyes bulging out from the effect of negative 'g', that I suddenly realised I had a problem: the aircraft controls felt wrong and movement was restricted. At once I tried to roll the aircraft the normal way up, but discovered that I was unable to move the control column to the left. My sudden sense of foreboding was reinforced when even an adrenaline-charged attempt to move the control column failed. I then pressed my left foot as hard as possible against the rudder pedal. The aircraft now began, slowly but surely, to roll away from inverted flight. However, once upright, and as soon as I centralised the rudder, the aircraft commenced an undemanded roll to the right. Immediately I re-applied my left boot which luckily checked the roll.

At this stage I needed to test, gingerly, the fore and aft movement of the control stick. Mercifully, the response in this direction seemed normal. Now I declared an emergency to air traffic control who cleared me to climb up to 10,000 feet, an altitude which would allow plenty of room for manoeuvre. On reaching that height I levelled off the aircraft and flew in a straight and level attitude. I had a chance coolly, and calmly to assess my situation. This did not take long. A rearward glance at the Lightning's ailerons at once revealed the root of the problem. The left aileron was in-line with the wing, as it should have been, but the right aileron was jammed in the fully up position. This explained, in an instant, the aircraft's vexatious tendency to roll to the right.

In view of the strong crosswind at Binbrook, I realised that a safe landing there was not an option. I calculated, therefore, that a diversion to RAF Coningsby, some twenty miles due south, would be my best hope. The runway at Coningsby was a long one and, of great significance, was more or less lined up into the wind. Having informed air traffic control of my plan, I was given priority clearance. I turned the Lightning onto a southerly heading and began a descent from 10,000 feet. En-route, I decided to carry out a slow speed handling check in the landing configuration. Having eased the control stick back to check my descent, I adjusted the throttles. As the airspeed reduced, I monitored the cockpit instruments with considerable care. Before long, I concluded that control was available down to an airspeed of around 185 knots – some ten knots above the usual speed for approach and landing. It would be touch and go but I felt there was at least a reasonable chance of a successful landing.

I checked-in with the controller at Coningsby whose voice sounded a little high-pitched. He was disconcerted, no doubt, by the disagreeable prospect of several tons of runaway machinery being dumped on his nice neat airfield. He read out the airfield's current weather information which confirmed that the all-important wind direction remained pretty much directly along the runway. He said that the local airspace had been cleared of all other air traffic.

So far so good. Now for my first attempt.

The flat Lincolnshire countryside facilitated the long, straight-in approach I had set up. A co-ordinated juggle of flight controls and throttles maintained the aircraft on a reasonable flight path and, as far as possible, I pegged the speed at, or just above, 185 knots. My eyes concentrated on the scene outside the cockpit, nevertheless regular glances at my flight instruments confirmed the crucial height versus speed ratio. At 500 feet, all seemed to be going quite well. At 400 feet, wind shear caused one wing to drop a little, quickly corrected by my left boot against the rudder pedal. By 300 feet the Lightning was on an even keel again. At 200 feet I felt ready to commit to a landing when the aircraft was suddenly struck by a violent gust of wind. This caused the right wing to drop away sharply and I knew that a landing from this approach was not feasible; I would have to overshoot and try again. As I pushed the throttles forward, simultaneously I applied maximum left boot to control the aircraft's turn to the right. At this stage the controller, his voice sounding most alarmed, pointed out that I was headed directly for the airfield's domestic site. He asked if I would try not to crash there. As politely as possible, I explained that I was attempting to do exactly that.

Now I flew a large, Bomber Command-type circuit to set myself up for a further long, straight-in approach. As before, I contrived to establish the optimum speed/height ratio. I was conscious of the complex variables, the perilous possibilities, but I wanted to persist. I was prepared to make last-second decisions; I would initiate another overshoot if necessary. *500 feet... hold her steady, Ross. 400 feet...watch for that wind shear...there it goes...anticipate...correct with left boot. 300 feet...should make it this time with any luck. 200 feet...shit...the wing's dropping again...* Immediately I advanced both throttles to commence a further overshoot.

As I flew away from the airfield for a second time, I speculated about whether to make a third attempt. Would this be realistic? Perhaps I should call it a day, settle for the inevitable Plan B, point the aircraft out to sea then, when clear of civilisation below, pull my ejection seat handle. I would come down on the end of a parachute, courtesy of Messrs Martin Baker. A valuable aircraft, however, would be lost. I glanced again at my fuel. I had 2,000lbs available, 1,000lbs in each of the port and starboard wing tanks; normally I would land with 800lbs in each tank. There was enough for another attempt. I decided, therefore, that I should make a third approach, but that if this attempt failed I would resort to Plan B.

The final circuit, similar to the last one, was another large Bomber Command-type effort to allow plenty of space. With the benefit of the two previous practices, this time I felt better prepared. The conditions, indeed, were similar to the other attempts except that at 200 feet I suffered no wing drop. 'Now's my chance,' I thought, and decided to continue down. Everything was fine until at the very last second, just a few feet above the runway, the right wing started to drop. Despite this, I felt that the aircraft was sufficiently under control and that the wheels were close enough to the runway for me to press on with a landing. I double-checked the cockpit indication of 'three greens' – the landing gear was down. I concentrated on the runway perspective. I closed both throttles. I was committed to landing. A last moment of vacillation, an awful awareness of risk, may have afflicted me, I don't remember. I do remember how a horrible pause was followed by a thump as the Lightning's right wheel and right wing tip both slammed onto the runway surface. The left wheel then touched down heavily, the landing parachute deployed and suddenly, as the jerk of the parachute began to slow the aircraft, I knew I had the machine under control. The landing had been less than ceremonious but I had made it. I was safely down. The machine had been saved.

Later, when I reflected on the episode, sober contemplation produced a curious mix of thoughts. The line between hero and villain can be a precarious one. However, events had worked out for me, I was pronounced more of the former than the latter, and I became the proud recipient of the Air Force Cross.

At the time, though, practicalities had to be considered. Explanations had to be given, forms completed, and telephone calls made. At length, I ended up with the small matter of how to return to my home base. My Lightning had been impounded by the engineers, I was a pilot without an aircraft. I would have to be driven back to Binbrook in an aircrew bus or a service vehicle of some description. However service transport, as usual, was at a premium, and I was asked to wait until something became available. This shouldn't be too long, so they said, meanwhile I should remain in the air traffic control tower.

I sat in a room there, by a window, and stared at the scene outside. The bleak March wind had gathered strength, just as forecast. On the far side of the airfield a brightly coloured windsock shook in the violent gusts. The aircraft hangars, set four-square against the Lincolnshire gales, looked invincible, solid, and doggedly determined. These were qualities I had needed. Nearby, a loose paper blown across the aircraft parking area darted here and there, chased by an airman; a crazy performance dictated by the whim of the wind. The clouds rushed by overhead. Engineers scurried about. My mind was preoccupied; somehow I seemed unable to concentrate. I was hardly aware of the chattering voices behind me in the room, though I remember turning round when the conversation became more animated. I didn't pick up the details, but I heard someone say: "Did you fancy your chances, then?" His colleague's mumbled reply was hard to make out but I saw him pull a face and shrug.

"It was touch and go, I reckon," he said. "Yes, touch and go."

Chapter 4

BATTLE
FLIGHT

PETER VANGUCCI IN GERMANY

Camouflaged buildings, great hangars, and the aerodrome's infrastructure were spread across acres of farmland in the area of Nordrhein-Westfalen, the most western, most populous, and most economically-powerful state in Germany. It seemed unlikely, hard to imagine at times, but just there, at the Royal Air Force base of Gütersloh where life in the 1970s appeared apparently peaceful and carefree, palpable danger meant particular preparations. For just a short distance to the east a manmade barrier, the iniquitous 'iron curtain' (more correctly known as the Inner German Border or IGB), stretched north and south in a near-900 mile barbaric, scandalous scar. Erected by the communist bloc in order to separate the West from the East, including the democratic state of West Germany from the Soviet-dominated East Germany, this curtain of iron was sacred. Crossing by land or by air could lead to dire consequences; even a minor incident could flare up into a major diplomatic row. Ultimately, World War Three could be triggered. Infringement of the iron curtain was a definite no-no.

The grim coldness of the Cold War may have been defined at Gütersloh but I had no crystal ball. The situation I faced on one tranquil Sunday in June 1973 could hardly have been anticipated. At the time, the deceptively quiet scenario, the warm weather meant some of us sat outside, seemed to induce a reflective mood. I would ponder, for instance, about how my cur-

31

rent situation was a far cry from the expectations, the dreams, and the un-tutored aspirations when I first joined the RAF. A far cry – an even further cry – too, from the days when, as a youngster in 1940, I had stared up at the sky to witness airborne dramas during the Battle of Britain. Dramas, in-deed, which had strengthened my growing determination to enter the RAF and to become a fighter pilot myself. The individuals who flew those Hurri-canes and Spitfires were, to me, icons and I longed to become one. I applied for pilot training and, to my very considerable relief and excitement, was ac-cepted. When this began, I soon learned the advantages of being versatile, resolute, even a touch eccentric. My family background had helped in that respect: my great grandfather, Alessandro Cesare Achille Vangucci, was a musician who, when he decided to move from Italy to England in around 1875, did not move alone. Nothing as straightforward as that for Alessandro. From the depths of Italy he brought with him the entire Royal Italian Military Band of which he was the conductor. They went on to play all over the south of England, including a performance for Queen Victoria, and a band which, over the years, eventually became the Bournemouth Symphony Orchestra. I liked to think that, notwithstanding a lack of musical association, Alessan-dro would have approved of his great grandson's activities.

At Gütersloh, where I was a squadron commander, I had to perform many and varied tasks for my squadron – 19(F) Squadron whose motto *possunt quia posse videntur* translated roughly into: 'they can because they think they can' – and for the administration of Gütersloh as a Royal Air Force station. Never-theless, I would aim to take my turn, usually on a Sunday, in the so-called Battle Flight shed where two Lightnings, fully-fuelled and fully-armed with two Firestreak infra-red missiles plus two 30mm Aden cannons, were kept at twenty-four-hour readiness. We were, if you like, sentinels of the West, gate guardians of freedom, or a quick reaction force in case of border problems.

So it was on that particular Sunday in June, a day of brilliant sunshine with hardly a cloud in the sky, that I was on Battle Flight duty together with another pilot from my squadron. Our accommodation, a small crewroom adjacent to a separate one occupied by ground crew personnel, was next to the special hangar that housed the Lightnings. As the morning progressed we were told that, since there was no sign of any activity near the border, a practice scramble would be planned for my aircraft sometime around mid-morning. This was good news. It would relieve the sitting around which, despite the day's sunshine, eventually became tedious. Furthermore, it would offer me the opportunity of an interesting and enjoyable flight.

Top: Course members at Hunter Operational Conversion Unit, 1966. *L-R:* Ted Girdler, Tony Craig, Les Howe, Dave Carden, Roger Colebrook. Standing at rear: John Aldington.

Left: Course members at Lightning Operational Conversion Unit, RAF Coltishall, 1965. *L-R:* Chris Mullan, Tony Ellender, Marcus Wills, 'Bunny' St Aubyn, Colin Bidie, John Hall (USAF), John Allison, Richard Pike, Kevin Mace, Jock Sneddon.

Below left and right: 226 OCU T5 XS449, Ed Durham pilot, 11th November 1966 (photo by Brian Farrer, sqn cdr).

Top left: Lightning formation 'break' into the circuit at RAF Akrotiri, Cyprus.

Top right: Four-ship Lightning formation flypast at RAF Akrotiri, Cyprus.

Above: Flight Lieutenant Roger Palin is about to inflate the dinghy in the survival pack and brief his unit on the use of items contained in the pack at Akrotiri. This was referred to as 'dry dinghy drill' and was in preparation for 'wet dinghy drill', where pilots were thrown into the sea with survival equipment. Great fun in Cyprus, but no laughing matter in the Tay estuary in winter!

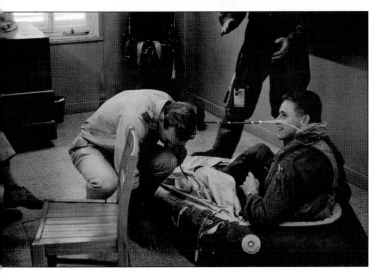

Top: Flight Lieutenant John May is the 'guinea pig' in the inflated dinghy, while Flight Lieutenant Roger Palin listens for a signal from the SARBE locator beacon. (Pilots had to notify air traffic control, prior to activating a live SARBE otherwise they would scramble a helicopter on the presumption that an emergency ditching had occurred.)

Middle: 56(F) Squadron members have dinner with the tanker crews at the Romantic Kebab Restaurant, Limassol, 1967.

Bottom: Cockpit photo of Roger Colebrook.

Top: Air Marshal Sir Edward 'Tap' Gordon-Jones KCB, CB, CBE, DSO, DFC, AOC-in-C NEAF, inspects 56 Squadron aircrew, 1967.

Above: Commander-in-Chief Air Marshal Sir Denis 'Splinters' Smallwood GBE, KCB, DSO, DFC, FRAeS, FRSA inspects 56 (F) Squadron in Cyprus, 1969. Chief Tech Bunn is standing next to F/O Roger Colebrook (in flying kit); Gp Capt Michael Beavis, OC Ops, partly hidden by AOC; Wg Cdr Bill Kelly, OC 56 Squadron (wearing black shoes); Flt Lt Paul Walters, 56 Squadron JEngO, second from right.

The practice scramble, we were told, would take place at some time after ten o'clock. This piece of advance information allowed a measure of mental preparation, however as we were geared-up to a five-minute time lapse between scramble order and becoming airborne, no further physical preparations could be made. Pilots were permitted to sleep at night – at least, attempt to sleep at night – as long as we remained in flying gear. This included flying boots and anti-g suit. It could seem odd climbing into bed – a bed made up with pristine white sheets – with size ten flying boots, but rules were rules and that was the way it had to be done. If the scramble alarm sounded, we had just to don our Mae West flotation jackets and bone domes as we dashed out to our aircraft, otherwise we were fully kitted and ready to go, day or night.

It was about fifteen minutes before ten o'clock on that morning when we were alerted by the shriek of the scramble alarm. Heartbeats promptly increased, adrenaline began to flow, minds raced as, automatically, we hastened into a well-rehearsed routine. As we rushed to the Lightnings, all of us speculated in our heads whether the controller was merely ahead of schedule, attempting to catch us off-guard perhaps, or whether this scramble might, actually, be for real. Within mere seconds I was in the Lightning cockpit, strapped-in, switches set, and raring to go. I checked-in with the controller via a system called telebrief, a direct telephone landline. Sometimes the controller would hold us at cockpit readiness while he briefed us, after which he would order "*scramble ...scramble...scramble...*" We then had just two minutes in which to start up the engines and get airborne. On this occasion, though, the controller gave me an immediate scramble order adding that he had an unidentified radar 'pop-up' at low level in the buffer zone. This, indeed, was serious. The buffer zone, almost as out-of-bounds as the border itself, was the final stage in an elaborate set of arrangements designed to prevent border infringement. 'Pop-ups' in the buffer zone were uncommon and invariably meant trouble...big trouble.

Well within the time allowed, I was clear of the Battle Flight shed as I taxied the Lightning at some speed along the short stretch of taxiway that led directly onto the runway. A breathless-sounding voice in air traffic control gave me take-off clearance. I turned onto the runway, made sure I was safely lined-up, and advanced both throttles to full cold power. A short pause ensued to allow the engines to settle, after which I selected full reheat on both engines.

There was a further pause, I heard a muffled boom-boom sound as the reheats lit, followed by a characteristic thump in the back as the effect of re-heat propelled me ever faster down the runway.

Airborne within moments, I quickly checked-in with the controller at 'Backwash'. This was the code-name for the GCI (ground control intercept) station manned by Luftwaffe controllers with whom we had an excellent working relationship. "Remain low level, vector zero-nine-zero and buster," ordered the controller. That meant head due east without climbing and do it fast. Very happy to oblige, I kept the reheats lit. Soon, though, with the aircraft close to breaking the sound barrier, I slipped the throttles out of re-heat and selected full cold power. "You're approaching the buffer zone now," said the controller, "start to reduce speed, turn right onto one-one-zero."

"Copied," I said, aware that the target was on my right side and that I was closing fast, too fast. I would have to be extra-vigilant.

"Turn further right now," said the controller in his highly-fluent but ac-cented English: "steer one-seven-zero and reduce your speed to 250 knots." At this, my speculation about the type of aircraft ahead began to narrow. Thoughts of a communist military machine, a hostile aircraft with, perhaps, a large red star painted on the side, one which might even forcefully resist my attempts to divert it back to its own side of the border, began to become less fanciful. "The target is now on your nose range two-and-a-half miles," said the controller. "Suggest you reduce your speed as much as possible."

I peered in front and to each side. On my left, the iron curtain seemed perilously close. The border itself, signified by small white markers often covered by undergrowth, would be hard to distinguish. Beyond, however, to the east of the actual border, lay the real iron curtain. The barbed wire, the dog runs, the minefields, the carefully-combed sandy strips, the flood-lights, the anti-vehicle ditches, the automatic alarms, the booby traps, the tall watchtowers manned by some 50,000 armed guards, all provided a more conspicuous, if meretricious, spectacle. I could almost sense the malicious, intrusive eyes of border guards staring at me through binoculars as they fol-lowed the Lightning.

Suddenly, I began to make out the rear profile of a small aircraft. The ma-chine was flying parallel with the border and, as warned by the controller, at a speed considerably less than my own. I eased back the Lightning's throt-tles and activated the airbrakes by flicking a switch. "Now visual with the target," I told the controller. Unable to reduce my speed any more, within moments I had caught up with the aircraft and was overtaking it. "It's a King Air," I told the controller, "standby." A twin-engine turboprop machine capable of carrying up to a dozen passengers, the Beech King Air was popular with amateur aviators and business operators. Certainly, the King Air in my sight seemed harmless enough. There were no attempts to evade, no red stars painted on the side, no signs of belligerence. Perhaps the pilot was lost. Maybe he had been overcome with curiosity. I noted the machine's registration, passed this to the controller who, after a pause, told me to exit the buffer zone.

The truth, I discovered later, was that the King Air pilot had obtained authority for a pre-arranged flight that Sunday afternoon to photograph a village near the border. It would be a one-off opportunity, he was told, with no second attempt. He had decided, therefore, that in view of the prescriptive conditions, a morning reconnaissance of the area would be beneficial. Unfortunately he had failed to tell the authorities of his plan.

When I landed back at base, a few people had gathered by the Battle Flight shed to see what had been going on. As often happened after a flight in a Lightning, I had a sense of job satisfaction. I was happy with the way the scramble had been conducted, I was especially happy to be told that I had set the record for the fastest time from crewroom to border. Flights in or near the border were fraught with hazard, however on this occasion I had helped to avoid too great a drama. From my point of view, the flight had been stimulating and worthwhile. I did not appreciate any form of boastfulness, indeed I actively discouraged it on my squadron, nevertheless I could not avoid a feeling of achievement. Alessandro surely would have been proud of me.

Chapter 5

PAPER TIGER?

*David Roome and 'his'
Lightning F6 XR773 on
the 74 Squadron dispersal
at RAF Tengah.*

*DAVID ROOME ASPIRES TO
BECOME A SPACEMAN*

I stared at the machine with a sense of trepidation. Owned by the United States Air Force, this titan-of-the-air was a record-breaker, certainly no paper tiger. A modified version of the USAF B-57, itself a licensed-built variant of the English Electric Canberra, the RB-57F had a wingspan approximately double that of the original Canberra B2. Because of this, the anhedral (or droop) of the monstrous wing had to be treated with particular caution on landing.

Even a small amount of bank at touchdown would result in the seven-foot fibreglass outer section of the wing being torn off. Furthermore, the unusual wing design meant that this remarkable aircraft had the bizarre requirement that airspeed on landing should, wholly contrary to normal practice, be three to five knots *faster* than the approach speed. As for power, the main engines each developed 18,000lbs of thrust – roughly three times that of the Canberra. As if that was insufficient, on each wing the RB-57F carried outer-podded engines each of which could produce 3,000lbs of additional thrust. The total engine power produced by this machine amounted to a massive 42,000lbs of thrust.

All of this meant unusual challenges for Lightning pilots like myself who were charged with the interception of the RB-57F. My story may sound apocryphal but exceptional circumstances placed me in an exceptional situation. Even though no suitable entry will be found in the Guinness Book of Records, to this day I still lay claim to a world record.

It was October 1968 when, as a member of 74 (Fighter) Squadron equipped with Lightning Mark 6s, and as an experienced Lightning pilot, I became involved with the RB-57F. My squadron members, based at Royal Air Force Tengah, Singapore, were briefed that interception of the American machine would entail specific techniques. When a RB-57F duly arrived at Singapore from its base at Yokota, Japan, I made a point of inspecting the aircraft on the ground. Along with a small crowd of others, I gazed at the ominous black nose-cone, the large round air intakes of the main engines, the podded engines further along the wing, and the vast, drooping wing it-self. With a sigh, eventually I walked away from the aircraft and tried to focus my mind on the job ahead.

The RB-57F's primary task on that visit involved high altitude turbulence trials. However, the United States Air Force had consented to an additional

RB-57F on the Pan at RAF Tengah, 1968.

mission (to use favoured American terminology) which would exercise Singapore's new, computerised air defence radar system. That was where I came in. The RB-57F would conduct a series of high altitude target runs while two Lightnings, one of which would be flown by me, attempted to intercept it. By that stage, all of those concerned understood only too well that this would be no easy matter.

Further briefings took place before, at length, the time of trial arrived.

The RB-57F took off just ahead of the Lightnings and set up for its first run at 50,000 feet. I carried out a successful intercept, then overtook the target from above; I just wanted to make the point that we Lightning pilots could operate in the upper atmosphere without difficulty. The target now turned through 180 degrees to set up for a second run. During this short turn, the pilot climbed up to 65,000 feet. This caused us some consternation when we realised that the RB-57F could climb to such an altitude in such a brief period of time. However, determined not to be daunted, the other Lightning carried out a further successful interception then, as before, overtook the target from above. The target now announced that he would perform one orbit before he commenced his subsequent run. This time he would be at 80,000 feet. It was my turn to carry out the interception.

At these high altitudes, I had to handle my aircraft with particular finesse. The requisite technique was to accelerate the Lightning to supersonic airspeeds at tropopause altitude (the boundary between troposphere and stratosphere, and the most efficient altitude for the Lightning's Rolls-Royce Avon 302 engines) then zoom up to the target's height for the interception. The tropopause, typically around 36,000 feet at European latitudes, was at its highest near the equator – regularly 55,000 feet or so. I would employ this to my advantage.

The use of supersonic flight meant, in turn, the use of reheat. However, with the aircraft's attendant high fuel consumption in reheat, I had to use the facility as sparingly and as effectively as possible. When in supersonic flight, delicate use of the flight controls was essential; the temptation to overcontrol could lead to wildly-inaccurate flying. Beyond Mach 1 (the speed of the sound barrier), the aerodynamic effect of supersonic flight masked the airframe buffet, but when at subsonic speeds, the least bit of rough handling at high altitudes would induce airframe buffet and loss of performance.

Despite these hazards, I accomplished a successful intercept of the target at 80,000 feet and I just managed to fly past the RB-57F at this altitude.

Now came the final test...the big one.

The RB-57F crew stated that they would need a little more time to prepare for their last run which would be at an unstated (i.e. confidential) altitude in excess of 100,000 feet. This was well beyond our capability and we had to admit defeat. Nonetheless, I had an urge to find the highest possible altitude attainable by the Lightning Mark 6. For this, I would have to accelerate the Lightning to its maximum airspeed of Mach 2.2 before commencing the zoom climb. To achieve that would require full fuel tanks and mine were far from full after the earlier supersonic runs.

It was at this point that Lady Luck played a crucial card. A Victor in-flight refuelling tanker en-route from Hong Kong to Singapore suddenly piped-up on the radio. "I've got some spare fuel," announced the captain of the Victor. "Any takers?"

"Sure," I replied at once. This was an incredible break; I wanted to stake my claim before anyone else got in ahead of me.

"Confirm your position," said the Victor man.

"North-east of Tengah," I said. "I've just finished an exercise with a high flying target in the supersonic zone."

"Should work out okay, then," he said. "I'll shortly be entering Malaysian airspace in that area." At this, I spoke very politely to the controller to gain his co-operation with my plan.

"Standby," he said. An apprehensive pause ensued; he was having a word with his supervisor, no doubt. "No problem," he continued after a moment, "your in-flight refuel has been approved." He then gave me a heading towards the Malaysian-Thailand border where I would rendezvous with the tanker.

My mind now began to work in overdrive. I calculated that, after in-flight refuelling my aircraft to full tanks, I should end up some 300 miles north of Tengah. That would offer me a clear line down the east coast of Malaysia. I would fly on a track that paralleled the coast on a heading towards base. The flight path would be well out to sea and therefore without restriction to supersonic flight. The situation looked ideal. Amazing!

The rendezvous with the tanker worked out well and, as arranged, I refuelled my Lighting to full tanks. When I broke away from the Victor tanker, I selected the throttles to the full cold-power position and initiated a climb to 50,000 feet – the Lightning's subsonic service ceiling. At that height, I rocked the twin throttles outboard and pushed them fully forward to select maximum reheat on both engines. As the Lightning accelerated through the sound barrier, I had to watch the Machmeter carefully: at these heights there was nothing outside the cockpit to offer an impression of relative speed. Mach 1.1...Mach 1.2...Mach 1.3... before long the indicator was edging up towards Mach 2.0. Now I smoothly, and rather gingerly, pulled back the stick. My eyes narrowed with anxiety as I monitored the attitude indicator: I aimed for a nose-up attitude of exactly sixteen degrees, the best climb angle (so we had been told) for that height and speed. By 65,000 feet I was beginning to lose performance. I therefore levelled off to allow the aircraft to accelerate once more. Amazed by the rapidity at which this occurred, I decided to let the Lightning have its head. The aircraft accelerated to its maximum permitted speed of Mach 2.2 at which I eased back the stick again. At 70,000 feet, with no loss of airspeed, I pulled back the stick to resume a sixteen degree angle of climb.

Now I was entering new territory – for me, at least. As the Lightning climbed up, unfamiliar symptoms, some of them subtle, some not so subtle, began to make me feel a little ill-at-ease. For one thing, in order to hold sixteen degrees of climb, I had to bring the stick further and further back. I put this down to a lack of downwash over the tailplane at such exceptional altitudes. Gradually, as the Lightning at last appeared to run out of steam, the nose began to drop and I was forced to level off. A quick check of my altimeter showed that I was just 200 feet shy of 88,000 feet.

I glanced outside the cockpit. The scene before me seemed surreal. Above, the sky was pitch black. To either side, the earth's curvature was clearly perceptible. This was an uncommon sight in those days (Neil Armstrong's moon landing was still a year or so away) and I felt awed, even humbled by such solitary opportunity. Over my left shoulder I convinced myself that I could see Vietnam. Ahead, the coast of Borneo was visible, on my right the length of the Malaysian peninsular pointed to Singapore, a tiny dot of an island. Beyond Malaysia, on my right, I could distinguish the coastline of Sumatra.

I took stock of my situation. The stick was now firmly on the backstops. I had no further elevator control other than to lower the nose. The ailerons, interestingly, were still very responsive. Both reheats had remained alight until I touched the throttles. When I rolled the aircraft and looked down vertically, I suffered a strange, disconcerting sensation – a bit like being balanced on the ferrule of an infinitely long umbrella. Suddenly I had the feeling that I did not belong up there. Musicians sometimes talk of how the music plays through them – is somehow separate from them, like an out-of-body experience. That day, up there, I could empathise. I wanted to get down. I needed to initiate descent. I therefore eased the Lightning's throttles back to the idle/idle position. This, however, triggered the warning bell in my headset which, in turn, gave me the one really fearful moment of the whole episode. The cockpit pressurisation warning had been set off. Quickly I tried to work out what was happening. I figured that a reduction in air output from the engine bleed had occurred when I closed the throttles. This had affected the cockpit pressurisation which, consequently, had placed the aircraft outside limits. With my pressure jerkin and anti-g suit I had some protection, but the Taylor helmet initially issued to the Lightning force for high-level work had been taken out of service. There was some oxygen overpressure fed to my face mask, though not very much. I realised that I was ill-equipped for safe flight at these extreme altitudes. Nonetheless, when I had worked out the cause of the cockpit warning I began to reason with myself that the situation was not as serious as first assumed. I decided, therefore, to adopt a very long, slow glide back to Tengah. As a secondary benefit, this would allow me to continue to enjoy the remarkable view.

A last bit of fun came when I spoke with Singapore Radar, a unit manned by RAF personnel. I was asked my height, to which I replied 'above flight level 450' (which meant above 45,000 feet). In those days, almost all controlled airspace ended above that height and I was not required, therefore, to divulge my actual altitude. The controller, however, became persistent as I was approaching an airway. Eventually, when I revealed that I was passing flight level 720, his reaction caused me considerable amusement. On reflection, I realised that that call provided the only independent evidence of my claim to fame.

Despite this, I now officially lay claim to the world altitude record of the Lightning – 87,800 feet. If anyone wishes to challenge this, let them speak now or forever hold their peace. As a serving member of 74(F) Squadron, I listened to a number of tiger tales (the squadron emblem was a tiger) – some of them authentic enough, some less so. My tiger tale may not be verifiable, and may not appear in the Guinness Book of World Records, nonetheless this claim, to the best of my belief, is no mere paper tiger.

Chapter 6

TIGHT
TIMING

*CLIVE MITCHELL
CUTS IT FINE*

It was nearly noon. The sun was high but cumulus clouds constrained the heat, a distinct contrast to the towering temperatures which, on occasions, we had experienced during a Cypriot noon. It could be hotter than hell out there in Cyprus as we stood near the hangar and by the parked Lightnings of our unit, 56(F) Squadron. Sometimes, out there, we would feel the hot air touch the inside of our lungs. We even learned that on the hottest of days it was better, cooler in fact, to close our lips almost and to take short, quick breaths. The sun would bear down on our shoulders, on our backs, and our shirts would offer scant protection. Perspiration would seep from our skin, trickle down our necks, over our chests and collect by the tightness of our belts which became damp and uncomfortable from the prickly heat on the skin. Here, at Wattisham in Suffolk, though, the sun's rays were less forbidding, the noon heat altogether more agreeable. It was the early part of 1975 when our squadron had moved from Akrotiri to Wattisham but it was over a year later when I became involved in the build-up to today's formidable plan. A plan, indeed, for which I was about to play a key part.

I looked around me. The landscape was flat, there was not a hill in sight. On a clear day in Cyprus, the pale-green lower slopes of the Troodos mountains would guide the eye up to the peak of Mount Olympus which, at 6,400 feet, provided a spectacular navigational aid for us Lightning pilots. I was the squadron's B Flight commander and I was proud of our achievements out there, of how we had worked hard to acquire high levels of operational effectiveness. I could remember our sense of shock when told of our fate, of how our days as a Lightning squadron were numbered. I suppose we knew it had to happen eventually, even so we could not avoid a heavy mood of disappointment. However, we were an experienced group by then and we became determined that, despite the news, we would uphold our professional standards to the end. In our hearts, though, we knew that we would miss Cyprus and the special lifestyle there.

Often we would start a day's work early in the morning and try to complete our planned flying programme before the noonday heat became too overpowering. I could recollect how, sometimes early in the day, I would look out from the squadron buildings with a sense of wistfulness. The sweet smell of orange blossom was pungent, birdsong was ubiquitous, the birds themselves flitted frantically here and there. I would look up into the sky and listen. Occasionally I could hear the faint pounding of the sea upon the beaches. In contrast with nature's scene, the black surface of the runway was a dark scar set between sandy-coloured grasses on each side. Later in the day, the runway, which pointed towards beaches and the waters of the Mediterranean Sea, would shimmer in the noon sun. On some occasions, near the squadron buildings, the heat would soften the tar and we would have to step carefully as we walked outside. Heat haze would hang like a vapour over the airfield. Such heat haze, however, was absent here at Wattisham and even though the plush Suffolk grasses underscored a calmer, less intrusive atmosphere, we still missed Cyprus.

I glanced at my watch. Timing was crucial, but there was time enough yet. I needed to remain vigilant but clear-headed, and dispassionate. The aerodrome at Wattisham was sited on prime farmland and beyond the airfield boundary I could see a farm tractor at work. Within the boundary, I could spot activity around a line-up of F4 Phantom aircraft. These machines belonged to 23(F) Squadron, recently-arrived, and they were the newcomers – upstarts – who were, in a way, the cause of all the day's excitement. I heaved a sigh. Before long, our own squadron would be converted to the F4 and those of our pilots posted to fly this American-built aircraft would need to learn all about a new machine, a two-crew machine at that. They would have to be taught about crew co-operation, and about how to work with navigators. A new mentality would be required. As Lightning pilots, we were used to self-reliance as we had to do everything: fly the machine; operate the radar system; fire the weaponry; navigate the aircraft; liaise with controllers; deal with emergencies. Now we would be expected to forget all of that, or at least much of it. We would have to discipline ourselves to discuss before we acted. It all seemed so alien. In the worst case, I feared that discussion could lead to polemic. We had heard rumours about some of the F4 navigators, how a number of them were failed pilots, had consequent chips on shoulders, and appeared overly competitive and career-orientated. Beyond the air force, there was not much call in the world of civil aviation for navigators trained to operate fighter aircraft.

"We're all set, sir." I turned round as the line chief called out. "Ready when you are."

"Thanks, chief," I said, and glanced again at my watch. I had signed the relevant paper-work, as had the other three pilots in our formation. We were as prepared as we could be and a few minutes remained before we needed to climb aboard our Lightnings. However, it seemed that the line chief was getting anxious. Perhaps we should get going now.

Once in the cockpit of my Lightning, I quickly carried out the pre-engine start checks. Then I looked across at the other pilots in our formation. When ready, each individual pilot gave me a thumbs-up sign. I acknowledged with a nod of the head and a thumbs-up sign of my own. I continued to keep a close eye on the time. If we started our engines too early we could become short of fuel; too late and we might miss our window of opportunity. I looked across at the air traffic control tower. Our own squadron man should be safely ensconced there by now, our squadron spy who would keep on top of things, and let me know of any significant changes of plan. The other pilots in the formation watched me carefully, as did the ground crews. All seemed on tenterhooks. I noticed an oil-stained cap half-poking out of a ground crewman's pocket. He'd better watch out, I thought, or that cap will become a loose article hazard when we start engines. I checked my watch again but it was still too early to start up. The virtue of patience, I knew, was needed right then; we should wait for another minute or two.

I thought back to the earlier briefing for the formation flight. There was a tension – a fine, high-drawn tension – in the room when I gave that briefing. I could see it on the faces despite outward attempts at blasé bonhomie. When I spoke, I aimed to be as concise as possible; I was conscious of the need for absolute clarity; nothing should be lost in translation. I described how, after start-up and take-off, we would head due east to a small quarry, a suitable ground feature over which we would fly a racetrack pattern. Meanwhile, by radio contact with our squadron spy in the air traffic control tower, I would be updated on events on the ground at Wattisham. Through binoculars, this man would be able to monitor our squadron's formal parade. This parade, held to mark our diamond jubilee among other reasons, would be attended by local dignitaries, air force chiefs, squadron families and friends.

As part of the proceedings, the 56 Squadron standard would be trooped in slow time along the front rank. This took some thirty seconds, the timeframe employed by the upstart 23 Squadron when, earlier in the year, they had held their own parade – a tight timeframe during which they had mounted a flypast of four F4s. However, for today's parade we were resolved to outdo our rival squadron. It was a matter of honour. We therefore planned not a half-minute timeframe – nothing as generous as that for our fine 56 Squadron – but a flypast that would coincide with the precise moment of the last movement of the parade's 'present arms' to the reviewing officer. Our timeframe would be restricted to a mere two to three seconds. At the very least, this was ambitious. If it worked, the plan, surely, would be record breaking. If it didn't work, well...

I sneaked a final glance at my watch. The moment, at last, had come. We should start engines now. I looked across at the other pilots, raised one hand and gave a distinctive circling motion to order 'start engines'. I could almost feel the palpable sense of relief that greeted this signal.

Before long, when the engines of all four Lightnings had started without snags, I received further thumbs-up signs from my fellow pilots. I called air traffic control and was given clearance to taxi for take-off. As I signalled my ground crewman to remove wheelchocks, I noted that the other pilots had done the same. We were underway. I taxied at a reasonable pace, but not too fast; I did not want the number four in our formation to have to race along in order to stay in position. I carried out my pre-take-off checks and called air traffic control again. "You're clear to line up and take off," responded the controller.

I had briefed the formation to take off in two sections, with two aircraft in each section. When the formation was lined-up on the runway, I glanced over my shoulder. All the Lightnings were in position. I concentrated ahead and gave a positive forward nod of my head. This indicated 'release brakes' to the other Lightning in my section. Steadily but firmly, I advanced my twin throttles to the full cold-power position. After a short pause, I gave another nod of my head: an order to 'light reheats'. The pilot following me, an experienced man, held his position with admirable, if typical, prowess and soon we were both airborne. As I commenced a turn towards the east, a further glance over my shoulder confirmed that the other two aircraft were following. Before long, we had joined up into a four-ship formation as briefed. So far, so good.

Shortly, as we approached the quarry, I ordered the other Lightnings to ease out into a loose formation while we flew the planned racetrack pattern. Close formation required acute concentration and I wanted to save our energies for the flypast itself. We flew at fairly low level, even so I could distinguish the suburbs of Ipswich to the south-east, and the Suffolk coastline beyond. The countryside around us, dotted with villages, held timeless appeal. Below, I thought I saw faces of walkers look up as the Lightnings flew by. A car pulled off the road and the driver got out to observe us, curious, no doubt, to know what was going on.

"Red formation, standby." This call from the air traffic control tower was a cue from our squadron spy. I recognised his voice at once.

"Go ahead with an update," I said.

"Standby for countdown," he said. My senses promptly heightened; I knew that action was imminent. At any moment we would execute Plan A and when we moved, we would have to move exactly as briefed. The time interval between the end of the spy's countdown to the moment of the parade's last movement of 'present arms' would be precisely one minute and forty seconds. I ordered the other Lightnings to resume close formation. Meanwhile, silence dominated the airwaves as I awaited the next radio call. Suspense built. The atmosphere, already filled with apprehension, became ever tenser.

"Red Leader, standby... countdown follows..." Our spy sounded harassed as he made this call. A further pause ensued, then: "Five... four... three... two... one... *execute*..."

I do not know whether, in my anxiety, my flying became rough at that point. I do not know if the others in the formation had difficulty in following me. Other than being the most intense period of concentration I have ever experienced in my life, I do not remember very much about the next one minute and forty seconds.

I do know that, shortly after the flypast and after we had landed, the commanding officer of 23 Squadron, Wing Commander Bill Wratten, came up to shake my hand. I do know that in the officers' mess later an air commodore approached me to say, an odd look on his face: "Surely it was a fluke?" I know also that the looks on the faces of the ground crews as we taxied-in after landing, the circle of approval with thumb and forefinger made by some of them, signified that our aim had, indeed, been achieved. The sense of relief, the sheer ecstasy of the moment, was felt by all. Perhaps this explains why, at that juncture, we failed to claim what must surely rank as a world record in time-planning. Maybe I should make that claim now.

At that stage, however, while I was climbing down from my cockpit, mixed emotions were rushing through my mind. When my feet touched the ground – literally and in a metaphorical sense – I looked up at the sky momentarily. Then I looked down again and noticed at ground level how the shadows of cumulus clouds advanced across the airfield – soft, subtle shapes which, for just a moment or two, I watched and wondered at. When I looked up once more and gazed skywards, I felt the need to pause for thought. I knew this was a day I should not forget.

Chapter 7

ULP!

*Rick Groombridge, on the left,
at the start of his exchange tour with a
French Mirage squadron.*

RICK GROOMBRIDGE APPEARS ALL OVER THE PLACE

The scene was set. 29(F) Squadron based at RAF Wattisham in Suffolk was getting ready for a first deployment to the Middle East. As we would have to in-flight refuel our Lightning Mark 3 aircraft while en-route, extra air-to-air refuelling practise with Victor tankers was organised. Although we did not forget the social side of life either.

The squadron pilots decided to hold a crewroom party two days before the date of departure. We wanted to bid farewell to families and friends. As we were setting up the beer barrels (which in those days had to be allowed to settle, then tested), a certain flight commander (commonly known as the 'Balding Crafty Jovial Flight Commander') entered the crewroom and said: "the boss needs someone to do an airborne radar check and it must be done today." Ulp! (i.e. help/gulp). He looked at me knowing that I had been the last one to get into the tasting session. "Gruntfuttock," he said (this was my undercover nickname though I was never quite sure why), "come with me." Oh dash it, I thought (or words to that effect), had I had two or was it three?

The flight commander's brief was simple. "Get airborne," he said, "and if the aircraft radar works, come back and land for a debrief. If it doesn't work, there's a rugby match at Coltishall so you can go up there and give it a bit of wiring."

I therefore got airborne, found that the radar didn't work (surprise, surprise) so – with great panache – went up to Coltishall for a bit of wiring. When I landed back at Wattisham I was debriefed by the Balding Crafty etc who paled when I told him what I had done. "My God," he said, "that was the Command rugby championships and the commander-in-chief was there." I spent two very worried days until I escaped to the Middle East and never heard any more about the matter.

More than relieved, shall we say, I was actually delighted when our flight to the Middle East got going. It was to be my first experience of a long in-flight refuelling sortie to the Mediterranean, but the flight proved to be not without problems. I was part of a formation of three aircraft – one Victor tanker supporting two Lightnings. All went well with the first two in-flight refuels as a result of which I became, perhaps, a little too relaxed. As we approached the spectacular vista of the Alps and as I began to marvel at the magnificence set before my eyes, maybe I got a bit carried away. In my defence, the experience of an Alpine tour by Lightning instead of through the limited porthole of an airliner seemed too good to be true. Anyway, after about ten minutes during which I 'danced the sky on laughter-silvered wings', I suddenly realised that it was about time to rejoin the formation. I looked around the sky. What formation? Not an aircraft to be seen. Where the **** were the others?

Suddenly it dawned on me that the others must have turned left at the French air traffic control reporting point of St Etienne. The tanker captain would have made a radio call but I must have missed it. Furthermore, the captain would have ordered a radio frequency change and I must have missed that too. I tried a nonchalant call to the tanker on my current frequency but without success.

I took stock of my situation. I was lost, and on the wrong radio frequency, I had no notion of the whereabouts of the rest of the formation, I had about ten minutes fuel remaining (quite good for a Lightning Mark 3) and I had little idea about the position of the nearest diversion airfield. At any moment I would have to revert to the emergency radio frequency with all the attendant embarrassment.

'Don't panic, Captain Rick,' I thought (these were the days before TV's Captain Mannering by the way), 'turn fifty degrees to your left and use your airborne radar.' Anyone who has used the Lightning Mark 3's airborne radar would know what a forlorn hope this was. Even so, I tried. I selected the twenty-five-mile scale. Nope...nothing. We had a sixty-mile scale which we all treated as a joke but 'needs must so here we go', I thought. Then, on the nose at a range of forty-five miles, I detected a fuzzy radar return. I realised it could be the 0845 Air France Caravelle out of Nice airport, but then again, what was there to lose? I chased after it at an airspeed approximately .0001 below the speed of sound (for I wanted to avoid a sonic 'boom' which might have upset the locals) when...oh joy! I began to make out the beloved silhouette of a Victor tanker (on second thoughts, it might have been a Valiant tanker – but who cares?)

I was quietly congratulating myself on my undoubted skills, panache, and craftiness (could it have been the good influence of the Balding Crafty etc? Nah, unlikely!) when I heard the tanker captain call: "You're clear astern the starboard hose."

A short silence ensued which allowed me to grasp that the message was for me. "Copied," I squeaked with as much composure as I could muster. I made it without further fuss even though this might well have gone down in the history books as the first ever supersonic rejoin on a Victor tanker. However, on reflection, that point seems fairly incidental.

The squadron's next three months in Cyprus involved ups and downs as might be expected. However, one incident in particular was, we could say, a *real* up and downer. It was towards the end of the three-month detachment and, as a parting gesture, it was decided that the squadron should undertake a nine-Lightning fly around the island. This, remember, was before the days of partition, the Cypriots were being especially fractious and our nine-ship, it was felt, might boost a few morales (although quite whose morale was never made clear).

Enter Gruntfuttock. The nine-ship took off as briefed, all was well with the world until, shortly after take-off...*CLANG...CLANG...CLANG*...a warning bell in my headset and a quick glance at my instruments showed that my Lightning was on fire. And not any old fire. A 'reheat one' fire – the worst

29 Squadron, taken in Cyprus, October 1968.

scenario. This was the feared emergency, one of the big ones. Thanks to the Lightning Mark 3's innovative fuel system, a 'reheat one' fire meant that an aerosol of high pressure fuel was spurting out between the fuselage and the ventral fuel tank. Loss of control was likely within about thirty seconds.

The drill under normal conditions was to point the aircraft in a safe direction and eject. No questions, no nonsense, just point safely and **** off. As simple as that. Or was it? The nine-ship had taken off from Nicosia airport, I was directly overhead a built-up area. If I ejected there I would clobber a lot of already-highly-pissed-off Cypriots and, oh yes, damage myself lethally to boot. I therefore opted to stay with the aircraft. I turned downwind and yelled "Mayday" on the radio. Air traffic control responded with admirable aplomb. The controller immediately ordered a taxiing Russian Aeroflot Classic airliner to hold its position. The Russian captain, however, ignored the controller and continued to taxi towards the runway for takeoff. Perhaps he saw 'USSR - 1, NATO - 0' on his score card. While he rumbled onto the runway the captain said: *"Ya nye ponimayoo."* Loosely translated, this means: "I do not understand."

As it happened, I had been a Russian linguist before I started flying. I therefore told the captain in good old-fashioned Russian: "take off, f*** off, do what you like but clear that ****ing runway fast."

"Ya nye ponimayoo," he replied. Surely my Russian was not that rusty, I thought fleetingly.

My already-limited options had become even more limited. I had no choice other than to fly directly over the airliner (which probably hurt the passengers' ears) and plonk my Lightning down just in front of Aeroflot and screech to a halt in the 6,000 feet that remained of Nicosia's 7,600 feet runway. Just as I was clearing the runway, Mr Aeroflot took off.

It was some time after our Cyprus detachment that 29 Squadron was sent on another ambassadorial mission. Perhaps we were considered experts by then. Anyhow, whatever the reason, we were chosen to undertake the very first squadron exchange with the Italian air force since World War Two. We were detached to Grossetto, an airbase near a Tuscan town of archaeological renown, although this aspect did not seem to feature highly when we were briefed by an Italian major from the base operations set-up. "We hear you Brits like beer," he said. "We got some specially for you." This prepared us well for a most civilised exchange (fly in the mornings then eat, drink and make merry) which appeared to part-explain the comment of a Luftwaffe officer: "For ze next war it is your turn to have the Italians."

The problem came when it was time to fly back to Wattisham. The weather across Europe was state 'red', i.e. terrible, but we were assured by the forecasters that conditions would improve from the north. On that vague promise, we got airborne only to find that the Italian controllers had not fired up ('surely the Brits would not be so "stupido" as to fly in this'). The Italians, it seemed, were not so daft after all, however neither were they in a position to join us up with our Victor tankers. After a lot of milling around at 36,000 feet and after a show of considerable initiative by one of our own tame controllers, a rendezvous was achieved and we were underway.

As we got closer to the UK it became evident that the hoped-for weather clearance just was not happening. Then, somewhere over France, the lead Victor tanker announced: "our base is state red so we'll have to leave now as we're at diversion fuel." Oh, spiffing! Promptly abandoned to our own somewhat unsatisfactory devices, we found the right frequencies, spoke to the right people, and eventually navigated our way up to Leuchars in Scotland. Luckily, the resident squadrons there (23 and 111) were very helpful and had a good laugh at our assortment of ill-fitting cast-off clothes worn for the three days it took for the weather at Wattisham to clear. *Buono viaggio!*

When, at last, we made it back to Wattisham, it was not long before I found myself on QRA (quick reaction alert) duty. As the QRA crew, we were the nation's front line of air defence while we waited with our fully-armed Lightnings ready to leap into the air at a moment's notice. Thanks to us, the rest of the country could sleep easy at night. Little be it said, but in truth a stint on QRA duty normally meant a twenty-four-hour period of sheer boredom. So it seemed that time. It was near Christmas, the Russian Tu-95 Bear aircraft were all in the woods, the M-4 Bison aircraft were out to graze, the Tu-16 Badger aircraft were in their setts.

Suddenly the operations phone rang. It was the duty controller. "Don't ask any questions," he said darkly. "Just do as you're told."

"Okay," I said. "Right-oh."

There was a pause. "An American exchange officer is about to visit you." Another pause.

"Okay," I said.

"You are to handover your duties to him then stand down to the officers' mess."

"Okay," I said. "Is that it?"

"That's it." No reason, no explanation, no nothing apart from a click as he put down the phone.

An American exchange officer duly turned up, I handed over to him as briefed. He was just as tight-lipped as the controller so without further ado I retired to the officers' mess to await developments. Soon, I heard a Lightning take off. It was a Saturday, there was no routine flying, so it must have been a QRA aircraft.

After less than an hour or so I heard the aircraft return and not too long after that the controller rang me in the mess. "You can resume your QRA duties now," he said.

"Okay," I said.

It was some time later when I heard on the BBC news a story about a USAF top-sergeant from the airbase at Mildenhall. This man's Christmas leave had been cancelled. On the pretext of a taxi test on a C130 Hercules troop-carrier aircraft, which he was qualified to do, he had got airborne and headed for the States, which he was not qualified to do. The Hercules had crashed into the sea off the UK.

Everyone was totally zip-lipped, nonetheless rumours abounded. Word leaked out that the Lightning that had taken off shortly after I handed over QRA duty eventually returned to Wattisham with only one missile. After landing, the Lightning had taxied to the airfield missile site before returning to the QRA hangar with the normal two missiles. I wondered about this. I have wondered ever since. If the speculation was true, and if for no other good reason, at least it would have shown that, for once, one of the bloody missiles had actually worked.

Heyho. Anyone for tennis?

Chapter 8

NOT AMUSED

ANTHONY 'BUGS' BENDELL CREATES A STIR

Superficially, the building seemed normal as I walked towards the wing commander's office. I soon began to realise, however, that any such initial impression was deceptive. As I entered the single-storey prefabricated building, I saw that the internal doors were askew, pictures hung away from the walls, and the walls themselves had been nudged sideways. Office lighting, which usually consisted of neon tubes suspended from the ceiling on chains, looked highly precarious: the chains had jumped off their hooks and the lights now dangled dangerously on the ends of electrical flex. I had to part these pendulous pillars as I headed for the wing commander's office and as I stepped past members of staff who, fortunately, seemed to take it all in quite good spirits while they swept up the mess.

Prudence dictated the need for a few ready-made excuses before I entered the wing commander's presence. So it was that, when I thought back, I reckoned that the problem must have stemmed from the morning's weather briefing. It was, in other words, the weather man's fault. The fellow had failed to emphasise that the recent change of air mass had introduced abnormally low ambient temperatures which were likely to affect engine performance. That would be my excuse, anyway – at least, one of my excuses. As I scratched my brains for further explanations – and rather better ones at that – I knew in truth that the weather conditions, other than the ambient temperature situation, had actually been quite good for my low-level aerobatic performance. This performance, indeed, had gone well as I worked towards my usual dramatic finale: a wingover manoeuvre followed by a high-speed run past the watching crowds.

For the event in question, I had been flying a Lightning Mark 1A. This meant, among other matters, one particular problem. In the early marks of Lightning, reheat ignition could not be guaranteed above an airspeed of 350 knots, although, once lit, the reheats remained stable throughout the speed range. Because of this, I always started my high-speed run from a steep wingover which involved an airspeed reduction to around 300 knots. When at 300 knots, I would engage both reheats before commencing a dive towards the runway. I would aim then to fly along the runway at about fifty feet, a height which precluded close monitoring of the aircraft instruments. I reckoned, though, that my speed should be approximately 600 knots as I flew abeam the air traffic control tower. On this particular day, because of the uncommonly low ambient air temperatures, the Lightning's Rolls-Royce engines had been more efficient than normal and the local speed of sound had been relatively low. The aircraft, I had to admit, had seemed to be moving rather fast as I flew past the control tower.

My first intimation that all was not well came from the controller who, in a rather higher-pitched voice than usual, made some comment on the radio to the effect that he no longer needed air conditioning. I thought he was joking but realised that trouble lay ahead when, after landing, I was met by my squadron commander. He looked shaken and said with a serious expression that I was required to report at once to the operations wing commander – with my hat on.

Unpleasant thoughts bounced around my head as I walked towards the wing commander's office. I was an experienced Lightning pilot by that stage, I should have been able to account for myself, nonetheless I could not avoid a sense of doom. Perhaps, this time, I had gone too far. Perhaps my air force career was about to be brought to an abrupt end. That would be unbearable, I reckoned. The air force had become my life; furthermore there was the small matter of how I would earn my living if they drummed me out of the service. As I walked along, fearing the worst, I recollected some of my early days in the air force. I thought about my service training. I had been one of the lucky ones – a young officer cadet selected, in the spring of 1954, to train in Canada. My initial flying, on the Royal Canadian Air Force Harvard aircraft, was at Moose Jaw over vast stretches of farmland in an aircraft that I found a joy to fly. I remembered how each student was issued with a parachute – hopefully to sit on rather than use. Because of my physique, a pillow had to be stitched to the back of my harness so that I could apply full rudder. That was just one of a number of health issues during my life, although naturally I was unaware at that point of the multiple sclerosis that would dog me later in life.

When at Moose Jaw, the students were granted mid-course leave and a group of us decided to head south for the west coast of the USA. The kindly father of one of the students lent us a late-model Packard and we crossed the border through Montana, Idaho and Washington State as we headed for Seattle then south to San Francisco. We could not afford motel accommodation every night, so a couple of our group would book in with the car while the others sneaked in through the back door. A single motel room shared between six people was hardly luxurious but at least it was just about affordable. The trick was to get out unseen the next morning.

In San Francisco, one of our number decided to find some women. He hailed a taxi and we all piled in like lambs to the slaughter. We were driven to a deserted warehouse where the yellow cab was exchanged for an unmarked black saloon. During the next ride some of us decided to hide our money in our shoes in case we were mugged.

At last we pulled up at a motel where the door was opened by a blowsy tart of mature years who greeted us in broad cockney: "'allo dearies." There were two girls on duty that night, we therefore had to wait our turn. The imagination ran riot as we waited. Would the woman melt in one's arms, return passion as two bodies ended up rolling together on the floor? Perhaps, while she clasped you to her and ran her hands about your body so that you became inflamed, her lips would be as hot as fire. She might bite her own lip and squirm with desire. You would tear her clothes away and tremble with anticipation. You would feel her breasts, her thighs. You would sense a madness within, a surge of...

The reality, regretfully, was less exciting. Furthermore, the girl I was with (she had emigrated from England a few months before) looked more than surprised when I had to fish around in one of my shoes to find the money to pay her.

For our next escapade, our group of six headed south again, this time for Las Vegas where we checked-in at the Kit Carson Motel. In downtown Vegas we watched old ladies feed silver dollars into slot machines; one of these ladies kept six machines going at once and became very tetchy if anyone disturbed her routine. At the blackjack and roulette tables there was no need for the casinos to cheat. With beautiful cocktail waitresses on hand to serve free drinks, and with no clocks or windows to distract, the gambler could stake bets to his or her heart's content and invariably lose in the long run. As I was below the legal age for drinking and as I was short of cash, I could not take full advantage of Las Vegas. This, though, was probably just as well: our Canadian buddies lost all of their money within hours of hitting town.

After further adventures that included visits to Salt Lake City and the Yellowstone National Park, it was time for us to recross the Canadian border and head back for Moose Jaw. We had covered over 4,000 miles in sixteen days, a journey that had been more than illuminating. For me, it had proved the trip of a lifetime.

I was, however, glad to return to flying the Harvard; Moose Jaw had become home to us, I was impressed by the Canadian instructors – they were first rate – and the course was going well for me. This was not the case, though, for all of the students and one of my friends was told that he had failed to make the grade. Another student was involved in an incident which caused considerable amusement at the time. This young man, as he approached the runway to land in his Harvard, was too high and too fast, as a result of which he overran the runway. His next radio call was heard by many:

"Moose Jaw tower, I've just landed and gone through a hedge."

"Oh dear," said the controller. "Is your engine still running?"

"Affirmative. The engine's still alive and kicking."

"Is it well enough to let you taxi back to the line?"

After a pause the student asked: "Do you want me to come back the same way or should I make another hole in the hedge?"

"Never mind," sighed the controller. "Switch off your engine and we'll come and get you!"

By the end of my time at Moose Jaw I had flown 185 hours in eight months – about average for the course. All the students were debriefed in alphabetical order but for some reason my debrief was delayed. I was the last student to be called in by which time I had convinced myself that I'd failed the course. Far from this, however, the staff announced that not only had I passed but that I had been awarded the Hawker Siddeley trophy for the best student.

From Moose Jaw I moved with my fellow students to the Royal Canadian Air Force base at Gimli where we would complete our advanced training on the Lockheed T-33 Silver Star. As we drove east to Manitoba, the weather got progressively colder. Gimli, a summer holiday resort on the shore of Lake Winnipeg, had that seedy, run-down appearance of a seaside resort in the off-season. Business was slow – so slow, in fact, that one barman allowed us to drink without proof of age. The experience, though, was hardly inspiring. We had to remain seated at a table as in Canada it was against the law to stand at the bar and drink. Furthermore, the beer was so bad that we had to add salt to help remove gases.

My first flight in a T-33, in January 1955, was a revelation. I had not flown jets before and, apart from anything else, I was unused to sitting on an ejection seat. The controls were precise and the T-33 lacked some of the Harvard's capricious habits. We could climb without fuss to the incredible height of 40,000 feet from where the winter landscape was a flat tapestry of grey-looking forest and white, frozen lakes – a bleak world far removed from the pressurised comfort of the T-33's cockpit.

The extreme cold at Gimli could produce unusual effects. On one occasion, with the outside temperature at a raw minus thirty-five degrees fahrenheit, I could recall how the first aircraft to take off in the morning had laid a carpet of frozen fog along the length of the runway. The aircraft engine had added just enough heat and moisture to disturb the delicate balance of the cold, soaked air and the result was spectacular – a ground-level version of the contrails produced by a high-flying aircraft.

On my first night solo flight at Gimli, I was struck by the brilliance of the night sky with more stars than I had ever seen before. I was at a height of 31,000 feet and about to commence a turn on a night navigational exercise when a sudden bright flash from behind lit up my cockpit. What the hell was that, I thought? On the radio, someone reported an explosion and air traffic control called each individual aircraft to check in. Only one man, a young French air force student on a solo flight, failed to respond. He might have ejected but nothing could be done until the morning. The following day a search aircraft found a hole in the ice on Lake Winnipeg. The hole had frozen over, but from the wreckage on top it was obvious that the French student had crashed at high speed. It was a sad day, he had been a popular lad within an ace of graduation. My own graduation came at the end of

March 1955 when, on completion of my advanced training, I was presented with my Royal Air Force pilot's wings by the station commander.

When back in the UK, I was re-trained on the Hunter aircraft which led to tours in Germany and Cyprus. In Cyprus, when I arrived at Nicosia in 1958 to join 66 Squadron, it was at a time when the Greek and Turkish Cypriots were at each other's throats. My squadron commander, Squadron Leader P E Bairsto was an odd, arcane man whose methods, if effective in the 1950s, would probably not be tolerated today. He greeted me with the words that he expected, "twenty-three hours and fifty-nine minutes of work in every twenty-four-hour period" and if I found that unacceptable "there were 500 pilots who would willingly take my place." This sounded a little extreme, nonetheless I enjoyed Cyprus and, despite the CO's edict, at weekends those of us not on duty would borrow a squadron Land Rover and drive north out of dusty Nicosia to the picturesque fishing port of Kyrenia. Vehicles on the Nicosia-Kyrenia road were targets for attack but the risk in broad daylight was considered low. Even so, we knew that nearby this very road a gang of Greek Cypriot lads had recently gate-crashed a dance held in a Turkish Cypriot village called Gönyeli. It was all thought to be good, harmless fun until folk became aware that the eight Greek lads had disappeared completely. The next day, a military patrol found a severed arm in a field. A subsequent house-to-house search of Gönyeli uncovered dismembered remains of the rest of the gang, and with an icy feeling of disgust enough to make the blood run cold we realised that the menfolk of Gönyeli did not make idle threats.

In mid-September of 1958 the squadron returned to the UK and the following year I volunteered to take on the commitment of Hunter display pilot. The Hunter was a splendid display aircraft: powerful; robust; and highly manoeuvrable even at slow speeds. In my routine, I included an inverted loop and an outside break – manoeuvres that induced red-out (the opposite of black-out) as negative gravity forces impacted on the body. The effect on the eyes produced that bleary-eyed, bloodshot appearance common to negative-g display pilots. For me, the most uncomfortable moment was when the aircraft first inverted and I fell away from the seat. There was always some slack in the harness even when a member of the ground crew had helped me to tighten the straps. All manner of doubts would flash through my mind: would the straps hold? Would I still be able to reach the controls? Would I finish up sitting on the cockpit canopy?

Even though I relished the task of display-flying in the Hunter, I found it physically exhausting. The aspect that appealed to me most of all, I believe, was the element of risk – living on the edge, if you like. However all good things had to come to an end, and by the latter part of the 1950s, the Hawker Hunter was beginning to show its age as an interceptor. Many of the Hunter Mark 6 aircraft were being converted to the ground-attack role, a job that did not appeal to me. The English Electric Lightning was about to enter service, and I rather fancied my chances on that aircraft. For some time I had nominated the Lightning as my preference for posting and I was delighted, therefore, when my posting notice came through: I was to become a flight commander on 111(F) Squadron.

In mid-July 1960, I reported to the Air Fighting Development Squadron at RAF Coltishall in Norfolk where, as one of the first pilots to be converted to the Lightning there, my course would be a one-off case. I was fitted with an anti-g suit, a partial-pressure jerkin, and an air-ventilated suit – the latter to help combat heat stress. I was measured for a Taylor helmet, a close-fitting helmet and collar, to enable pressure breathing above 56,000 feet. I was strapped like a helpless blue beetle into an ejection seat rig with sensors attached to wrists and ankles to record my pulse and blood pressure. I also was put in a special chamber to simulate explosive decompression from a simulated 22,000 feet to 56,000 feet in three seconds. I spent eleven hours in the flight simulator, I went through extensive ground school lessons before, finally, I was ready for my first Lightning flight. This would be a solo flight; a dual-control version of the Lightning had not been produced at the time.

For that first flight I had been extensively briefed, nevertheless I was caught off-guard by the rate of acceleration on take-off. This resulted in a nose-wheel lift-off speed of 150 knots achieved well within ten seconds of brake release. I sympathised with the comment of one wag that he was 'with the aircraft all of the way until the moment of brake release for take-off'. Once airborne, I found the Lightning to be positive on the controls throughout the speed range and remarkably docile at low speed in the airfield circuit. The circuits were marginally wider than in the Hunter and I found the touchdown speed of 165 knots noticeably quicker.

I spent several more months at Coltishall, where morale was sky-high in the excitement of the Lightning's introduction there. Then, in mid-December 1960, I moved south to Wattisham in Suffolk to join 111(F) Squadron. However, it was not until February 1962 that I finally received a chance to workup as a Lightning solo display pilot – an ambition I had nurtured since Hunter days. I was well aware of the demands: any fool could beat up an airfield but serious practise and precise judgement were needed for an impressive aerobatic demonstration. This was emphasised in dramatic manner by a potential display pilot on 74 Squadron who, having lost control while attempting a Derry turn, flicked into a flat spin. Immediately he engaged reheat, which probably saved his life. Even so the normal three-second delay before reheat light-up caused the Lightning to descend so low that flames from the reheat set fire to the airfield grass. Less fortunate was Alan Garside, the pilot who took over the solo aerobatic slot from me. Some months after he took over, Alan was tragically killed when his display sequence went wrong.

The g-limits on the Lightning, both positive and negative, were lower than on the Hunter, I therefore found the Lightning less physically demanding. I soon discovered how to use the Lightning's excess power to advantage. For example, it was possible to perform a square loop by replacing the conventional smooth flight path with sharp corners. I would descend vertically and then, with no apparent chance of recovery, apply power at the last moment which caused the aircraft to change direction abruptly. In another manoeuvre, I would hold the Lightning in a level steep turn at 350 knots (an ideal display speed) balancing induced drag against full power. With this technique, I would never exceed 5.5 'g' and it was possible to complete a noisy 360 degree orbit well within the airfield boundary.

As the display season progressed, I started to collect modest fan mail. One gentleman, who appeared to know a thing or two about flying, wrote to say that, until he had witnessed my Lightning display at Stansted, he had been convinced that the Spitfire was the last true fighter aircraft in service. I felt quite pleased about that. I wondered what he would have made of today's saga. I knew, however, that the time had come to put such thoughts to the back of my mind as I approached the last part of my walk of destiny. Above, I observed a small, magnesium sun that hovered and glowered through thin layers of cloud. Dark trees on the far side of the airfield lined the horizon. The wind was still brisk but for one of the few times in my life I shivered physically from something other than cold.

When I entered the building where my fate would be decided and as I walked past the dangling light fixtures and the members of staff quietly sweeping up the mess, I had an ever-growing sense of foreboding. My future was in the balance. Through clouds of dust that still polluted the air I spotted the wing commander's office. I hesitated for a moment before entering. When, eventually, I summoned the courage, I knocked timidly on his door. A shaky voice told me to enter. I stood and stared as I went into the office. The wing commander had an intense, animated air. His expression of horror and rage seemed to confine me to the caprices of the dark. He raised his arms and tried to speak but he twittered like a bird in the jaws of a cat. He's completely off his trolley, I thought. His blue air force uniform, now covered in a layer of white dust, was barely recognisable. From a desk drawer he produced his wing commander's hat, the only part of his uniform protected from the dust and consequently reasonably normal. He placed the hat on his head. With a perfectly straight face he cleared his throat and managed to say in a distinctly nasal twang: "I suppose you thought that was funny, Bendell."

I stared at his pale face, its colour now barely distinguishable from the new hue of his service uniform. His stalwart attempts to formalise the interview, to give me an almighty rocket, somehow added to the comedy of the situation. Perhaps he expected me to say a curt "no, sir, not at all," but all I could manage was something along the lines of "well, sir, now you come to mention it..." I struggled to stifle a spontaneous guffaw.

"You've caused a hell of a lot of damage, you know, Bendell."

"I'm sorry, sir."

"The air traffic control tower's bloody well falling apart at the seams, at least six huge double-plate glass windows have been shattered, the locals are going berserk, the camp cat's probably had a heart attack. Let alone all of this..." he waved a hand around his office. "Even the bloody weather man's been knocked off his sodding perch. The fellow keeps going on about his barograph."

"That's terrible, sir." I tried to sympathise but in truth I wanted to throw back my head and laugh.

"What the devil went wrong?" he persisted.

I attempted to explain.

"Shit," he said.

"Indeed, sir."

"Somebody will have to pay."

"I know, sir. Her Majesty, perhaps?"

"It's not funny," he said for the second time. He drummed his fingers on the desktop and seemed at a loss for further words. "You'd better get the hell out of here now," he said eventually.

"Yes, sir." I saluted, turned round and as I walked from his office I listened to his parting rant: "Her Majesty will not be amused, Bendell, I want you to understand that..."

Chapter 9

BASKET CASE

John Walmsley climbing into the cockpit, January 1968.

JOHN WALMSLEY RECEIVES MORE THAN HE BARGAINED FOR FROM A VICTOR TANKER

A pilot might make a Mayday emergency radio call just once or twice in a flying career. Such a call is not made lightly. Normally, but not always, transmitted on a special radio frequency, a Mayday call will cause listeners suddenly to sit up, heartbeats to increase, and emergency services to react. Derived from the French *m'aidez* ('help me') the call, re-served for situations of grave and imminent danger, means that all other radio traffic on the frequency must cease, other than those assisting with the emergency. Individuals who make frivolous Mayday calls, or who interfere with these calls, will have to justify themselves and may even end up on the wrong side of the law.

In my own case, a Mayday call was far from frivolous and, unlike many an emergency state, was not the result of a series of errors or, as can happen all too easily, a build-up of unfortunate events. I was, one moment, in a situation of good order and control until, within seconds, all hell let loose.

It was the morning of St Valentine's Day 1967 – a day which had started well enough, although if love was in the air I was probably too busy to have paid it much attention. I was a new pilot, with less than 200 hours on the Lightning, and I had been programmed for a sortie of in-flight refuelling. The aim of the flight, for which I would act as leader of a pair of Lightnings, was to exercise my abilities in a new-found art: that of flying in close formation against a wire basket attached to a fuel hose trailed behind a Victor tanker. This was a particular skill which, for the inexperienced, could be quite unnerving at first. Throughout training, when pilots learnt how to hold close formation on another aircraft, any form of physical contact with the other aircraft was most definitely discouraged. Unlike cases from World War Two when, in extreme circumstances, some pilots deliberately rammed an enemy aircraft, in peacetime this was not considered a good idea. For airborne refuelling, however, pilots had to overcome natural aversion and force themselves to strike another machine intentionally – albeit with a basket and hose arrangement some distance from the host aircraft.

An added complication for the pilot was the basket's tendency to move away from the Lighting's refuelling probe at the last instant. This was caused by local airflows. The refuelling probe, positioned just below and to the left of the pilot's eye-line, had a built-in weak point so that, in the event of trouble, the probe end would break off. For most pilots, the best technique was to focus the eyes on the Victor tanker ahead while peripheral vision kept contact with the basket. An ill-advised tactic (for the majority, at least) was to stare intently at the refuelling basket: gross over-control could be induced all too readily with consequent failure to place probe within basket. An unwritten rule stated that, as the need for fuel became more urgent, so the pilot's level of desperation (and probable defeat) grew exponentially. This became increasingly evident in conditions of flight turbulence when the refuelling basket was inclined to bounce around like a lunatic creature.

Once good contact between probe and basket had been achieved, the tanker crew would operate a switch to allow fuel to flow from tanker to Lightning.

My squadron, 5(F) Squadron based at Binbrook in Lincolnshire, was equipped with the latest mark of Lightning at the time – the Mk 3 ER (extended range). This aircraft, with a large non-jettisonable ventral fuel tank, and kinked and cambered wing leading edges, was soon designated the Mark 6 (interim) pending re-equipment with the full Mk 6 version with strengthened rear fuselage, arrester hook and an overwing fuel tank capability. My flight that day, in Lightning XR755, was planned in reasonable weather conditions with some medium-level cloud. During the pre-flight briefing we were told that the Victor tanker would deploy its centreline hose instead of the two wing hoses. This was unusual for us, but no great problem.

On completion of the briefing, the other Lightning pilot and I walked out to our respective aircraft. The take-off went as planned and during climb-out I was able, between patches of cloud, to observe the Lincolnshire Wolds around the airfield at Binbrook. This early part of the flight, with its prospects of interest and adventure, always seemed a good moment for me. The flight planning, the briefs, the aircraft preparation – all had been completed, now was the chance to convert plans to practice. At the time I was focussed, nevertheless I would reflect later how, as a schoolboy, I had always wanted to fly. I would recall how, on completion of my basic and advanced pilot training, I had been at once thrilled and astonished to be offered that most enviable of opportunities – to become a Lightning pilot, even though I was still a mere teenage lad.

Clear in my memory, too, were recollections of my first faltering steps as a rookie pilot on the Jet Provost trainer. I could remember how the complex array of knobs and buttons in the JP cockpit had seemed so bewildering that sometimes my mind had gone blank. The gulf between those early days and the stage of flying one of Her Majesty's fighter aircraft had appeared, at times, so wide as to be almost impossible to bridge. My first attempt at aerobatics, on a day with walls of cotton-wool white cloud that towered on either side, had felt intoxicating. My instructor had demonstrated a slow roll, then it was my turn. I had pushed the stick forward during the roll but not enough to prevent what had felt like a screaming spiral towards earth. My initial attempts at formation flying had also been erratic – I was close to the leader at one moment, then miles away the next. The concept of two aircraft flying adjacent to one another at speeds of hundreds of knots could take some getting used to. Gradually, though, I had begun to improve; bit by bit my aptitude had been nurtured, my confidence had developed. It had taken time, but eventually I had built up to the standard needed for today's in-flight refuelling exercise.

As we continued our climb-out, I glanced at the other Lightning and then, as was routine for any good fighter pilot, checked above and below and all around for other air traffic. Below, the Lincolnshire countryside, a mix of soft green and gaunt bleakness, stretched uninterrupted towards the coast. On our left side, to the north, the Humber estuary, lined by the conurbations of Grimsby, Immingham, and Hull, provided a distinctive navigational feature. Mablethorpe, a small coastal town known chiefly, I reckoned, for the tired, left-over air of a seaside resort in winter, was to our right. As we crossed the sandy coastline, with the North Sea spread beneath us, I spoke with the GCI (ground control intercept) controller. He gave us a new heading and told us to continue our climb. The Victor tanker, said the controller, was in position and our rendezvous would proceed as planned.

Before long, as we levelled at around 30,000 feet, I could obtain a useful overview of events. The bulky form of the Victor tanker meant that, with my airborne radar switched on, a good return appeared on the small radar screen at eye level on the right side of my cockpit. With this radar picture, and with information provided by the ground controller, I felt confident enough to make an early 'Judy' call on the radio (no further assistance required from ground control). After a series of turns with the other Lightning in a flexible 'battle' formation, we closed from astern onto the Victor tanker. The Victor's captain instructed us to hold on his port side while he deployed the tanker's centre refuelling hose. This was prudent: it was not unknown for the hose brake to fail and for the heavy hose to break away from its housing.

This day, however, the hose mechanism seemed in order, the large refuelling basket was settled in the correct position and I was cleared by the tanker captain to move astern the basket. I called the captain when happy with my position at which he said, "standby" shortly followed by "you're clear to refuel."

I now eased the Lightning's twin throttles forward and manoeuvred judiciously to guide the aircraft probe towards the refuelling basket. I had to fly with finesse. As a matter of pride I was keen for success on my first attempt. While I drew closer and closer to the refuelling basket, my reactions by this juncture in spontaneous sympathy with the basket's movement, I reminded myself to relax; it was too easy to become overly tensed up. I concentrated on the recommended technique: eyes focused on the Victor tanker, peripheral vision noting the refuelling basket's position. For the last few feet before contact, I used just one throttle to reduce the temptation to over-control the engine power. The centre basket, normally reserved for bigger, bomber-type aircraft, loomed ever larger but still I resisted the temptation to stare at it directly. Normally, one of the few times to flout this rule was at the very last stage when a small but satisfying clunk told me that the probe had made contact with the basket. At that point I glanced quickly left to confirm positively that the probe, indeed, was settled in the basket. Then I looked ahead again and checked the coloured lights on the Victor tanker. These lights, situated at the rear of the aircraft next to the refuelling hose, changed from red to green when fuel had started to transfer successfully.

At the same time as I monitored the Victor's refuelling lights, I glanced occasionally at the Lightning's fuel gauges. When the gauges showed that the Victor had delivered the requisite amount of fuel (normally to full tanks) I eased back one of the Lightning's throttles and aimed to sever the connection between probe and basket. I was mindful that the Victor's hose, as it trailed from the rear of the tanker, followed a natural curve in the airstream. If I withdrew the probe at a bad angle, this would cause the fuel pipe to jerk violently up or down. That day, though, the procedure went smoothly enough and, for exercise, I was cleared by the tanker captain to make a further contact before the other Lightning took over. This, too, went well and it was not until I had started to back off from the second contact that I experienced a sudden sense that something was wrong. It was a seminal moment. There was no brilliant white light, no neon sign, more a quiet awakening of some arcane sixth sense. I felt, perhaps, a peripheral consciousness, as if walking down a dark alley with the gradual realisation that a malicious presence had started to follow; a sensation that can cause the hairs to prickle on the back of the neck.

This sensation, however, quickly changed from hunch to harsh reality when the malicious presence manifested itself in the form of the Victor's refuelling basket. A hasty glance to my left revealed that the basket was now sheared from its hose and firmly stuck on the end of my Lightning's refuelling probe.

Events now began to happen fast. The Lightning was still level with the

Victor's hose just as the latter developed an erratic, vicious oscillation of considerable violence. The side of my aircraft received several ferocious thwacks at the same time as the Lightning was deluged by a massive cloud of fuel. Later, my colleague reported that my aircraft had been engulfed within a ball of fire. I was unaware of this myself, although I had lost sight of the Victor tanker in the cloud of fuel. Immediately, I initiated an emergency break-away to the left from where I could take stock of my situation.

I soon realised that the refuelling basket, still firmly attached to the Lightning's probe, was creating so much extra drag that my aircraft now yawed excessively to the left. However, with the application of my right boot on the rudder pedal and with maximum right rudder trim, I was able to control the yaw. I therefore turned away from the Victor tanker and towards base while the other Lightning flew towards me in order to inspect the outside of my aircraft. Meanwhile, as I gingerly tested the new flying characteristics of XR755, I reduced engine power to initiate descent. Shortly after this, cockpit warnings of aircraft electrical failure illuminated. I changed at once to the radio emergency frequency to declare a 'Pan' urgency call. As I did so, I noticed another light flicker on my warning panel: my number one engine oil pressure was low. Suddenly the penny dropped. The electrical problem was not caused by generator failure but by engine failure. Both of the engines had died on me. Lightning XR755 was now a glider. Moreover, few would argue that the Lightning probably made the world's worst glider.

This, without doubt, was another seminal moment. There was a good chance that I would have to make use of my Martin Baker ejection seat, furthermore I knew that I was beyond the range of the Whirlwind search and rescue helicopters. With the prospect of a long, cold wait in my dinghy in the middle of the North Sea, I had no hesitation in declaring 'Mayday' on the radio. As I made the call, simultaneously I closed both engine fuel cocks. This procedure, which did not appear in any of the manuals, would, I hoped, drain surplus fuel from the engines and thus facilitate relight. By now, with XR755 gliding like a brick, I had lost half of my original height and was at an altitude of around 16,000 feet. I took a deep breath and with fingers firmly crossed attempted to relight one of the engines. This, happily, turned out to be a moment of eureka: the Rolls-Royce Avon engine relit without hesitation. I advanced the throttle to bring the generator back on line then, as I pressed the second engine's relight button, heaved a further sigh of relief as this engine also fired up successfully. Perhaps, after all, I was not destined to die this day.

GOOD SHOW

FROM

FLIGHT SAFETY

John Walmsley was awarded this certificate having displayed considerable
flying skill after suffering the double flame out and making a successful
precautionary landing.

The remainder of the flight proceeded without incident except that I
elected to land at Leconfield, the nearest suitable airfield. My home base of
Binbrook was not far away but under the circumstances I wanted to land
without delay. After I had landed and when there was an opportunity to reflect on the incident, on the fine division between success or disaster, I realised that I had visited some dark places in my mind. A Whirlwind
helicopter, which had been scrambled following my Mayday call, flew me
back to Binbrook. The Whirlwind then took off again to return to its home
base. As I waved a farewell 'thank you' to the crew who waved back cheerily,
I began to walk slowly towards my squadron buildings. I felt as though a
load had slipped from off my shoulders and down to the ground.

Chapter 10

'SHOULD BE A DODDLE'

Colin Wilcock and John Anders,
with a 5 Squadron Mk 6 in the background.

COLIN WILCOCK
RETURNS XR755 TO
BINBROOK THE
NEXT DAY

Apart from vague impressions, or snatches of conversation, I don't remember much else about the morning. Not beforehand, anyway; not until it happened. There may have been one or two visitors present in our 5 Squadron crewroom, I don't recall, but I suspect the room was occupied mainly by squadron pilots like myself. Binbrook, after all, was a remote place and we saw few others apart from occasional visiting aircrew. For those of us there that morning, I'm sure a keen topic of conversation would have been John

Walmsley's in-flight refuelling experience of yesterday. It was an incredible, worrying event for which I for one, as a mere twenty-one-year-old rookie pilot on the Lightning, felt completely shocked and unprepared. Double engine failure on the Lightning, as far as I was concerned, just did not happen. Such an occurrence was certainly no part of the intensive and costly training which I had completed recently courtesy of Her Majesty's Royal Air Force.

One thing I do remember was that the weather was reasonably good although the wind was quite strong that day. The windsock was made to stand out straight, like a signpost, but that was normal for Binbrook. Also normal was the crewroom's calm atmosphere, although I was a little too relaxed, perhaps, when the duty operations officer poked his head around the door. "You're just the chap," he said as he fixed me in his stare.

"I am?"

"Transport should arrive here before long to drive you over to Leconfield. XR755 has been cleared by the engineers there so I want you to fly the aircraft back to Binbrook."

"Okay."

"It'll be a fifteen-minute flight; should be no problem."

"Sure."

By the time I had collected my bone dome and other flying gear, the aircrew bus, as promised, had turned up. I told the operations officer what was going on and soon I was on my way to Leconfield. When I got there, and when I spotted Lightning XR755 parked in front of a hangar ready for the short flight back to home base, I saw at once that the Victor tanker's in-flight refuelling basket from yesterday's incident had been removed. The Leconfield engineers had found no damage to XR755's airframe or engines. And the aircraft, they said, was fine although there had been no opportunity for them to start up the engines for ground checks. Before getting airborne, therefore, they wanted me to test the engines when I was positioned at the end of the runway.

As part of my pre-flight walk-around checks, my inspection of the air intake was more thorough than usual that day, nonetheless I could see no sign of damage. At least, I don't remember seeing any sign of damage. One thing I do remember, though, was the ground crewman who helped me to strap-in to the Lightning cockpit. I don't know why I should recollect this, but he was oldish – or so it seemed to a twenty-one-year-old, anyway – and he looked as though he had spent his life helping to strap-in aircrew. With a bone dome on my head we could not converse but his expression seemed to say: 'Be careful. There isn't any sense in not being careful.' I could not reply, of course, but when I was fully strapped-in, and when he began to step down the ladder attached to the cockpit side, I gave him a thumbs-up sign as if to say: 'Don't worry. I'll be okay. Should be a doddle.'

The start-up and taxi seemed to go normally, so I asked air traffic control for permission to line up on the runway to check the engines. Once there, I ran up each engine in turn to around 80% power – the maximum I could hold before the brakes started to slip. Again, all seemed in order so I asked for clearance to take off. This was given without delay and, as I wanted to double-check everything, I quickly ran through the pre-take-off checks once more. I remember, in particular, the flap setting: there were no intermediate flap settings in the Lightning – the flaps were either up or down. To reduce my lift-off speed to around 180 knots I ensured 'flap down' was selected. This would mean the use of reheat and, although there was no proof, even with hindsight, the influence of reheat could hardly have helped what was about to happen.

The initial part of the take-off appeared normal. I set off down the runway, selected reheat at the appropriate moment, and eased back on the stick as the aircraft approached 180 knots. The nosewheel lifted off. Within seconds the mainwheels followed. Then, suddenly, I realised there was a problem. This was a moment when some people, apparently, might 'freeze-up'; a split-second when the computer system between the body and the brain could go wrong: the brain wanted to know what was happening and needed instructions but the system couldn't cope. For me, thankfully, this did not happen. Perhaps it was my training; perhaps it was instinct; perhaps it was a sense of sheer survival. Perhaps, after all, I had a guardian angel looking after me that day. Whatever the reason, I found myself able to act swiftly, and coolly.

Just after lift-off and just as the whole aircraft began to vibrate quite severely, I knew there was no time to waste. I cancelled both reheats immediately and raised the flaps and undercarriage. By now fairly convinced that the engines were the source of vibration, I throttled back each in turn. As one of the engines (I forget which) seemed to cause more vibration than the other, I shut it down without further ado. At this stage I was flying over the River Humber with Binbrook ahead. Aware of the potential of a Martin Baker let-down I re-tightened my seat straps as much as possible, looked ahead for good clear areas over which to point the aircraft before I ejected, and momentarily felt for the top and bottom ejection seat handles to confirm, in my mind, their position. I made an emergency radio call and was cleared by Binbrook for a priority landing. The vibration persisted as the airfield loomed, and the possibility of an ejection remained firmly at the forefront of my thoughts. My worst fears, however, were not realised. I managed to land the aircraft, and I even managed to taxi clear of the runway. From that point, though, the aircraft was handed over to the engineers.

The results were a cause of considerable amazement. The engineers peered again into XR755's air intake but, as there were still no signs of damage, they decided to carry out ground tests. During these tests, both engines seized. Clearly, deeper investigation was required; it was time to call in a representative of the manufacturer, Rolls-Royce. Both engines were removed and stripped down. Then the experts found, at last, the root of the problem. Of the sixteen stages of XR755's Rolls-Royce Avon 302 axial flow engines, the compressor blades were missing from about stage eight onwards. When we had inspected the front of the engine through the air intake all had appeared in order; the goings on at the back end, though, were a different matter.

The man from Rolls-Royce said that I was lucky not to have suffered a sudden fire or worse. The cause of the damage, he reckoned, was the ingestion of fuel when the Victor tanker's hose had broken. A gradual degradation of the engines had meant that by the time I landed at Binbrook the Avon 302s were ready, as the saying goes, to give up the ghost. They did not, however, and they managed to keep going. I, too, managed to continue – another twenty-two years of fast-jet flying, to be precise, during which time I never had to eject from my aircraft.

Perhaps, that day, I really did have a guardian angel in attendance.

Chapter 11

EARLY DAYS

BRUCE HOPKINS GETS STARTED

I think it was the uniform, as they say, that did it. The zip-pocketed, blue uniform blouse worn exclusively by members of the Lightning force was, in those days, a sign that I had made the grade. A sign, indeed, that made me feel about ten-feet tall. Even so, I had a sense of foreboding, a sense that new rules were about to be written, novel boundaries broken. The ground crewman that assisted me that day as I entered the Lightning cockpit to strap-in was a man of few words, nevertheless I was aware of his apprehension, the anxious shake of his hand. This was understandable, I suppose. All of us were affected by a general sense of excitement and as I prepared, on that mid-May day in 1960, for my first flight in a Lightning aircraft I was certainly no exception.

Before the flight I had studied Lightning pilot's notes avidly and I had spent several hours in the flight simulator, although these hours, while helpful, could never act as a substitute for the real thing. With two operational tours under my belt, on Venom and Hunter aircraft, and having accrued some 1,600 flying hours, I was a reasonably well-experienced fighter pilot by then. I was, nonetheless, keenly aware of the need to tread warily as I entered new territory with hidden hazards, and arcane prospects. As a two-seat version of the Lightning was not available at that stage, there would be no one to hold my hand at the start, no one to guide me through the first few flights. I would be on my own from square one, just as many of the fighter pilots in World War Two.

That war, which had ended a mere ten or so years before I joined the service in the 1950s, still had a potent influence on most aspects of life. Even as late as 1953, for example, sweets remained rationed. In the area of fighter tactics, the Battle of Britain continued to shape our thinking. Still serving in the RAF were men like Al Deere, who had been shot down seven times, baled out three times, and collided with a Me 109. One of his Spitfires at an aerodrome was blown up 150 yards away by a bomb, and another of his Spitfires exploded just seconds after he had scrambled to safety. If we talked about such mind-boggling events, we discussed other aspects too, including the complex issue of personality – or more accurately expressed, perhaps, the paradox of personality, of how, in war, the unlikely characters were sometimes the ones who shone the most. The case of Bob Doe, the RAF's joint-third most successful pilot in the Battle of Britain, illustrated this. By his own admission after the war, Bob Doe lacked confidence when he began flying, he disliked aerobatics, especially inverted flight, and he only just passed the tests to gain his pilot's wings – an inauspicious start for a fighter pilot. On Hitler's so-called *Eagle Day* in mid-August 1940, the twenty-year-old Bob Doe was on duty with 234 Squadron at Middle Wallop, Hampshire, when his squadron was ordered airborne. Years afterwards he recalled: "I thought I was going to be killed. I was the worst pilot on the squadron." As he took off, he was filled with dread. He feared the thought of death, but he feared even more the thought of being branded a coward. One hour later, when he had landed from his first sortie of that day, he had shot down two enemy fighters. Four of his ostensibly 'better' colleagues had failed to return. Just a few weeks later he was one of only three left of his squadron's original complement of fifteen pilots.

The Hurricanes and Spitfires and the men who flew them in the Battle of Britain remained legendary, but we knew that, with Hispano cannon and Browning machine-guns about to be superseded by infra-red missiles and pilot-operated radar, a complete re-evaluation of tactics was needed. Aircraft performance, too, was in the process of metamorphosis. For instance, even though, in February 1952, a Spitfire Mark 19 of 81 Squadron in Hong Kong had achieved an altitude in excess of 50,000 feet and a reported speed of Mach .96 in the ensuing out-of-control dive (which, although unconfirmed, was reckoned to have been the highest speed ever recorded by a propeller-driven aircraft), such parameters could be surpassed with ease by the Lightning. There was a new global order now; the Battle of Britain seemed a world away; modern fighters like the Lightning were about to fashion a revolution.

One aspect, however, would remain much the same. Some marks of Lightning, equipped with a gyro-based PAS (pilot attack sight) and two 30mm Aden cannons, would be reduced to this somewhat rudimentary form of armament when, presumably, the aircraft's two missiles had been expended. In that case, the tactics of close air combat would have to be employed; lessons from former Hurricane and Spitfire pilots would be applied, albeit in modified form. The fundamentals of good lookout, of spotting the 'Hun in the sun' before he spotted you, of techniques in a 'circle of joy' combat, would endure. The Lightning's in-built radar might help in the initial search, but once close combat had commenced, use of airborne radar in a single-seat fighter could prove more of a hindrance than a help. In close air combat, the fighter pilot, whether in the cockpit of a Spitfire or a Lightning, would need to move his head ceaselessly from side to side, up and down, and all around until, from force of habit, his attention was focussed almost entirely outside the cockpit. Occasionally, and without ceasing the movement of the head, the pilot would glance at his aircraft instruments. The glance would take no more than a second and record, like a camera, a dozen things at once. At the speed of the camera shutter he would note fuel contents, oil pressures, oxygen, altitude, airspeed and other data. Then he would look outside again, and search persistently for a small black speck that might turn into a life-size enemy aircraft.

If this happened, and the pilot was faced with an enemy machine close up, the trained pilot would steel himself, prepare his machine, and continue to watch the other closely. He would carry out pre-combat checks. Still watching the enemy, his hand would move instinctively, delicately around the cockpit. He would ensure his PAS was switched on, he might adjust the brightness, he would be ready to flick from 'safe' to 'arm'. In two years time, on an in-service trials sortie to fire a telemetered Firestreak missile against an unmanned Meteor drone target, this point would be brought home to me in a vivid, if embarrassing, manner. In these trials, for the first time, Firestreak missiles from Lightnings would be fired against targets. The count down would go well, the cameras would be activated, and I would enter the firing bracket. However, when I pressed the firing trigger, nothing would happen. The sortie had to be abandoned while we investigated the cause of the problem which turned out to be finger trouble. Despite all of the training, the copious briefings, and the simulator exercises, I had forgotten to move the final arming switch from 'safe' to 'arm'...

"Okay, sir?" The ground crewman leant forward as he mouthed these words. By now strapped-in to the cockpit of Lightning DB (development batch) XG336, I turned to double-check that my Martin Baker ejection seat safety pins had been removed and stowed. The ground crewman then gave me a thumbs-up sign as if to say: 'Good luck! You're on your own now.' I nodded by way of thanks and watched him as he stepped down the ladder.

I experienced a mix of feelings. I seemed to have a heightened awareness of minor things, issues which normally would not have bothered me. Perhaps, with the senses sharpened by an imminent period of intense concentration, there was a natural tendency for this. As the ground crewman struggled to remove the cumbersome cockpit ladder, I glanced around. The air force base at Leconfield, from where I would conduct the flight, looked less than spectacular. Dreary hangars, acres of taxiways, and military buildings stood stark against the promise of the spring day. The air traffic control tower, which later earned a reputation as a haunted building after the tragic death of a young flight lieutenant on the base, looked typical of such structures. Beyond the airfield boundary, the East Riding of Yorkshire held alternative attractions. Once I was airborne, the Humber estuary and the distinctive curl of Spurn Head would provide good navigational aids. Not that I was unfamiliar with the local area. Since my posting to the Air Fighting Development Squadron (AFDS – a trials and tactics unit within the Central Fighter Establishment) at the beginning of 1960, my first few months had been spent at RAF Coltishall in Norfolk. Four months later, however, we had moved to Leconfield while the Coltishall runway was upgraded. My task during that period had been to fly a 'chase' Hunter aircraft every time a Lightning got airborne. The Lightning, treated with kid gloves in the early days, flew with a chase aircraft in the vicinity in case the Lightning pilot needed help. As a regular 'chaser' I was reasonably well-acquainted with local landmarks around Leconfield.

For today's flight, it would be my turn to be 'chased'. I felt honoured, indeed, that my 'chaser' would be a very experienced fighter pilot, Flight Lieutenant Ken Goodwin, who would be in a Hunter Mark 6 aircraft. He had taken off ahead of me in order to climb up to an altitude of around 8,000 feet before the Lightning got airborne.

Once airborne, one of my worries would be that of aircraft serviceability. The serviceability record of these early Lightnings was poor – to put it politely. In time, though, I would look back with some satisfaction (gratitude, even) that I had suffered no serious problems during my first flight, or for some months afterwards. However I suppose it was inevitable that this would not last.

In mid-December 1960 I will be flying a trials sortie in Lightning XM138 when, suddenly, I'll feel a heavy thump on the airframe. At once, I'll check the aircraft instruments and test the flight controls. I will be aware of an elevator control restriction so I'll ask the pilot of a nearby Javelin aircraft to inspect the Lightning's airframe. The pilot will report nothing amiss, but as my elevator control will remain limited I'll opt to head for base and a straight-in approach to Coltishall. By expeditious use of the elevator trim, I will achieve a successful landing. Shortly after touchdown, though, all hell will be let loose. A cockpit fire warning will appear, simultaneously the controller will yell that I am on fire. I will hastily clear the runway and close down the engines. As rapidly as possible I will switch everything off in the cockpit, unstrap and stand up. When I turn around, I will see a flame of some twenty feet spring from the fuselage and I'll spot fire trucks race towards the aircraft. Later, as I reflect on the incident, I will recall a distinct lack of hesitation in my ensuing actions – a leap from the cockpit followed by a run like hell.

The subsequent unit inquiry will reveal that a hot gas leak during my flight had affected a contiguous fire bottle. The fire bottle had exploded, bent the adjacent elevator control rod and fractured a fuel line. As a consequence, fuel had collected in the bottom of the fuselage. The reduced airflow after landing had allowed the fuel to ignite. Lightning XM138 will be a write-off.

Other memories of my time with AFDS will include a successful firing of a Firestreak missile in May 1962. Unlike the previous occasion I remembered to place, with considerable care, the final arming switch from 'safe' to 'arm'. The telemetered Firestreak fitted to my Lightning had no explosive and was designed to miss the target by a safe margin. Despite this, the Firestreak scored a direct hit on the Meteor drone aircraft which broke up and fell down in flames. I had shot down my first – and last – aircraft. In future, a remote-controlled Jindivik aircraft would be used with a towed heat source as a lure for the infra-red Firestreak missile.

These tests and events – unfamiliar, innovative, and enthralling – would provide the basis of operational procedures for 74(F) Squadron, the first RAF squadron to be equipped with the Lightning. When, in 1988, the Lightning retired from RAF service, the fighter was credited with the intentional shooting down of just one aircraft – ironically, a British machine – although some might argue the point (see Chapter 7 – Editor). (This shooting-down followed an incident when a Harrier pilot ejects from his aircraft but the Harrier, pilot or no pilot, continues to fly quite happily). Considering the number of Luftwaffe aircraft (nearly 1,800) reckoned to have been shot down by the RAF in the few months of the Battle of Britain, this statistic may seem poignant, even ludicrous. However, while some will view the use of public funds and effort as grotesquely wasteful, others will point out that the ultimate upshot of the Cold War, for one thing, might have been rather different without the focus of such funds and effort.

By 1988, the Lightning's gentlemanly treatment ended. Nearly 350 of them were built, but the machines' pampering of the early days was well and truly over. Some Lightnings will become 'gate guards', some will suffer at the hands of scrap metal dealers. Despite the aircraft's quirks, most pilots who will have flown the machine, including me, will retain firm loyalty and fond memories.

In mid-May 1960, however, all of this lay in the future. My immediate task just then was to complete the pre-start cockpit checks safely. When satisfied that everything was in order, I looked up. The dreary hangars, the acres of taxiway, the military buildings provided a sombre backdrop. The ground crewman stared up at me. His expression was impassive but his stance – his whole body language – suggested that, as he stood there clutching a fire extinguisher, he was still quite nervous. In that respect, I thought, he was not alone. I raised one finger and made a circling motion. The ground crewman replicated this signal. I was cleared to start Lightning DB XG336's first engine. My flight was underway.

Chapter 12

RUSSIAN ROULETTE

JERRY PARR'S LONG-RANGE SCRAMBLE

A high-level contrail, a single, welcoming white streak in the sky revealed what I judged to be the Victor tanker's position. The sign seemed like a salutation. I had just been scrambled by ground control and as I rushed to fire-up my Lightning I was in a state of high excitement. The task was urgent and I knew that the Victor tanker's support was crucial – without it, my mission could not be accomplished. Despite its might and bluster, the Lightning was an impotent machine on long-range sorties unless offered in-flight refuelling support. I was about to undertake such a sortie and I was heartened to spot signs of what I reckoned would be my own personal, private Victor tanker.

Earlier, when I had arrived that morning for a period of duty at the so-called QRA (Quick Reaction Alert) hangar, the weather man's prognosis had revealed mixed messages. At my base of RAF Leuchars in Scotland, the weather was fine, and the sky was clear of cloud. To the north and west, however, towards Iceland and the area known as the Iceland/Faroes gap, a meteorological depression signified that the weather prospects up there were distinctly gloomier. As I mulled over the implications of this and as I went, together with my fellow 23(F) Squadron pilot, to check over the two aircraft ensconced in the specially-designed hangar, I had no inkling of what may lie ahead in the next twenty-four-hours of QRA duty.

The Lightnings in the QRA set-up were fully-armed machines available all year round, day and night. These aircraft, with dedicated pilots and ground crews, would respond as required by the ground controller who received instructions from above. Ultimately, this might mean the highest levels of government. From time to time we received scramble orders to intercept aircraft, including Soviet bombers, although such sorties tended to be spasmodic. In reality, a twenty-four-hour period of QRA duty could mean twenty-four hours of boredom for pilots and ground crews.

When the other pilot and I had checked our separate aircraft and set the cockpits to our individual needs for the quickest possible getaway, we returned to our small QRA crewroom adjacent to the engineers' room. As we waited for the call which might never come, we listened to the radio (including the recent Abba number which, having hit the high spots, was being played almost non-stop), discussed flying and squadron affairs, and talked about life in general. It was mid-May 1974 and remarkable things were happening in the world at large – there was talk that the US president might be impeached, and at home our extraordinary prime minister had taken unprecedented power following the hung parliament after the general election in February. When conversation on weighty subjects began to flag, my colleague and I might read or, by mutual consent, switch on the TV. In quiet moments I would wonder about my wife. We had been married for less than a year and I knew that, though stalwart, she was inclined to worry about her husband and his somewhat outlandish line of work.

It was in the middle of such musings that the telebrief crackled into life. This device, a compact and unobtrusive box placed in one corner of the crewroom, connected us directly with the ground controller at RAF Buchan (a radar station somewhere in north-east Scotland). By that point it was mid-morning and the telebrief's raucous message intruded on our quietude. The controller advised us that two so-called zombies (Soviet aircraft) had been spotted by Norwegian radar. The zombies, flying in formation, had turned onto a south-westerly course and were headed our way. Despite our interrupted peace and quiet, the news, for me, was welcome. As QRA 1, I was due to be scrambled first; my colleague would act as back-up in case of problems with my aircraft. Unless the zombies turned away, my day would change abruptly from being very dull to very absorbing.

The Buchan controller had suggested that, with plenty of advance warning, time should be on our side; the scramble order, if it came, should not happen for a while yet. I was an inexperienced pilot at that stage in my career, nonetheless I had learnt that radar controllers, like weathermen and second-hand car dealers, should be taken with a fairly large pinch of salt. So it was on that day. Despite his hint, it was not long before the controller piped up on the telebrief once more – this time with an anxious edge to his voice. "Alert one Lightning," he said. As I flicked a switch to set off the scramble alarm, all on QRA duty dropped what they were doing. Everyone now rushed towards the two Lightnings. The ensuing mêlée could seem chaotic but the procedures were well rehearsed: each man knew precisely what was required of him.

Within moments, I was seated in the cockpit of my Lightning. I plugged in my headset to speak with the controller, and simultaneously I was helped by a member of ground crew to strap-in. I had to be slick, professional, meticulous. It was during these proceedings, as I chanced to look up briefly, that I spotted that contrail painted across the sky, which signified, I reckoned, a Victor tanker scrambled ahead of me. This gave me a warm feeling. My flight, destined to be a prolonged one, had been provided with the necessary support. If I was to engage in Russian roulette, at least I would be suitably facilitated. I glanced across at the other Lightning whose pilot sat there ready to take over if needed. When I was safely airborne, he would probably be stood down by the controller.

"Vector zero-two-zero, scramble…" the controller now ordered me airborne. I placed the switches 'gang bar' up, opened the high pressure fuel cocks and, one at a time, pressed the engine start buttons. I gave a hand signal to the ground crew to remove the external power source and the wheel chocks. I removed the basic but effective wooden prop that ensured the canopy was kept open. Then I operated a switch to close the canopy and I pushed the locking mechanism fully down. Before long, as I taxied out into the sunshine and as the Leuchars air traffic controller cleared me for immediate take-off, I went through the pre-take-off checks. When satisfied, I taxied directly onto the runway and selected full cold power. I paused to allow the engines to stabilise, then I selected full reheat on both.

My rendezvous with the Victor tanker did not take long and soon, as we flew together in loose formation, we were headed north for a long transit flight. The Victor's wingspan, at over 100 feet, was more than three times that of the Lightning yet the erstwhile nuclear bomber did not look especially large from my airborne perspective. I speculated on the Victor crew's airborne chat. With five members of crew versus just me on my own in the Lightning, I imagined that a good crew would enjoy plenty of repartee. Perhaps I felt lonely. I could even imagine myself as a sixth member of the tanker crew, albeit a remote one. It would be good to join in their banter, to appreciate a link other than mere fuel systems. I imagined the crew as they relished a cup of air force coffee and a sandwich while each man sat at his allocated station in the Victor. I wondered what they would be like, these five men whose sole job at present was to support me. Each, no doubt, would have his own role, his own concerns, his own take on the situation. Like me cocooned inside a warm cockpit, probably little thought would be given to the hostile environment immediately outside, the freezing temperatures, as each man, surrounded by control panels, monitored his own rows of dials, focussed on his own part in the crew's overall task. It struck me as unfortunate that, despite our regular work with the Victors, members of the Lightning force rarely had opportunities to get to know their tanker colleagues.

I glanced at my fuel gauges. As my ventral tank was nearly empty by now, I decided to ask the tanker captain for a refuel. I felt that frequent top-ups would be prudent in case problems suddenly developed with either aircraft. Anyway, regular refuelling would help to keep me occupied and alert. "You're clear astern the port hose," said the captain in reply to my request.

I enjoyed practising the art of in-flight refuelling. The key to success, as taught to all pilots from square one, was to close on the tanker by formating on a steady reference point. Over-concentration on the flight-refuelling basket itself, especially when the thing started to bounce around in turbulence, was likely to lead to trouble. The basket, some three feet in diameter at the open end, was designed to guide the receiving aircraft's probe into a refuelling nozzle at the basket's end. Once contact was made, a small advance of one of the Lightning's throttles was needed to ensure a leakproof contact between nozzle and probe. Simultaneously, the Victor's refuelling pod would wind-in automatically. This, theoretically at least, should take up any slack in the hose and hence impede any probe-damaging ripples along the heavy hose. In practice, though, not all undulations were stopped and the hose and basket were seldom steady, even in smooth air. On completion of refuelling, the Lightning pilot needed to reduce engine power and slide gently backwards. The wrong technique meant the Lightning could be seized by turbulence from the Victor's wing and hurled outwards. Sometimes, when backing-off, the probe-tip could refuse to disconnect properly, in which case – with the possibility of the basket and a length of hose still attached to his aircraft's probe – the Lightning pilot had a problem.

That day, however, all went well and I soon resumed a loose formation position on the Victor. As we continued to head north, I began to notice changes in the weather pattern. Wisps of high level cirrus had started to thicken and I became aware of a gradual increase in flight turbulence. The Victor captain announced that he intended to climb up to 35,000 feet to keep us above the worst of the weather, meanwhile the ground controller at Buchan confirmed that he still had radar contact on the zombies. Evidently, there was no sign of them turning around; an intercept, therefore, was likely. With this news I felt a prompt thrill of anticipation; it seemed that I was about to be required to earn my keep.

Some hour or so after my take-off, the Buchan controller told me to standby for important information. As I waited, I gazed at the cloud layers which continued to build up around me at all heights. After a pause, the controller said that the two zombies had begun to fade from contact on his radar screen. This suggested that the Soviet machines, following a fairly predictable routine, had descended to low level and thus out of Buchan's radar contact. Hastily, I made a few back-of-the-envelope type calculations to estimate the zombies' likely position in about thirty minutes time. I topped-up to full fuel, waited around ten minutes, then bade farewell to the Victor captain. I added – with a somewhat plaintive note, no doubt – that I hoped to see him later. He wished me good luck and confirmed that the Victor would remain in the vicinity to refuel the Lightning after my intercept.

As I reduced engine power to initiate a descent to low level, I entered an area of dark, forbidding cloud with embedded heavy rain. At 5,000 feet, with my flight instruments indicating a fairly rapid descent, I decided to ease the rate of descent, although I held my planned heading. Confident that my calculations would work out, I felt quite relaxed in a warm, comfortable cockpit. However, when I was down to an altitude approaching 700 feet, harsh reality promptly struck. At that height, as I broke cloud to find myself scudding around amongst endless acres of low stratus cloud, it dawned on me that my altimeter, even though on the correct local area setting, had been highly misleading. When I had flown towards the low pressure system near the Iceland/Faroes gap, I had relied on the altimeter's accuracy. However, the wretched thing now indicated some 2,000 feet even though my actual height was nearer to 500 feet. With an involuntary shiver, I realised that if the cloud-base had been at surface level I would, in all probability, have flown straight into that cold, grey, storm-tossed sea. I had not been married long, yet sheer chance, or maybe my guardian angel (who knows?), anything but skill had saved me from an ignominious disappearance without trace.

With ominous thoughts bouncing around my head, I reflected for a second or two on past ground school lessons. Perhaps I should have been more attentive when lecturers had pointed out the woefully boring, nevertheless true, information that altimeters tended to over-read during descent towards areas of low pressure. But this was no time for inner demons to haunt my solitary situation. I struggled to put superfluous matters to the back of my mind; I forced myself to concentrate on the task in hand. Two large blips had appeared on my airborne radar screen and, as they marched from right to left across the screen, I calculated that the targets would cross ahead of me at a range of some five or six nautical miles. I therefore advanced both throttles and aimed ahead of the targets, a tactic that resulted in my rolling out some two nautical miles behind them.

Before long, as I closed up from astern, the distinctive outline of two TU95RTs, otherwise known as Bear D aircraft, started to come into view. The Bear D, that veritable icon of the Cold War, looked big, ugly, and brutish. 'Bear' was indeed an appropriate sobriquet. The pair that I now approached continued to fly near to each other, although not quite in close formation. To me in my single Lightning fighter, these Soviet machines appeared formidable and menacing. With a wingspan of some 165 feet, four massive turboprop engines and, under the fuselage, a large bulge that housed an airborne radar, the Bears often flew in pairs. The crew appeared to be equipped with dark leather World War One-type flying helmets as if borrowed from the Red Baron himself. Their image may have seemed comical, but at times the crews' behaviour could be manifestly uncomical.

Sometimes the Bear D pilots would slow down suddenly or swerve dangerously in attempts to throw off interceptors. At night, the Bear D crews
would shine strong flashlights into the eyes of interceptor pilots.

As, tentatively, I drew up alongside one of the Bears, I spotted the tail-
gunner ensconced behind a perspex window in a cramped-looking compartment on the fuselage side. I wondered if the fellow would wave, maybe
hold up a girly-model type picture, perhaps something else to signify my
presence. He seemed, though, fairly docile and I was unaware of any particular reaction. I speculated whether these two aircraft were Cuba-bound,
a common routine, so it seemed, as the Soviet bloc sought to sustain links
with Fidel Castro's communist regime. With a crew of ten (double that of
a Victor tanker) the Bear Ds had plenty of personnel on board. Such a
large crew on such a long flight, I mused, would need significant quantities
of rations. Perhaps they cheered each other up with the odd tipple of
vodka.

By now, as ever in a Lightning, time began to press. A glance at the
cockpit gauges confirmed what, from my on-going mental calculations, I
knew already: fuel was getting short. I noted the tail numbers of the Bears,
performed a positive break-away and initiated a climb. A quick call to the
Victor tanker was answered by a comforting voice, presumably that of the
Victor's navigator, who gave me a suggested heading towards a rendezvous
point. The tanker crew, as ever, had performed their task with admirable
efficiency as they kept track of my movements. As a result, the rendezvous
was swift and before long my Lightning's fuel gauges had started to move
in the desired direction. I stayed in company with the Victor for around
forty-five minutes until, when sufficiently close to Leuchars, I thanked the
crew and said I would leave them. After a final top-up of fuel, I waggled
my wings in salute, moved well clear of the Victor, then engaged full reheat. The Lightning now accelerated through Mach 1.0 towards Mach 2.0
and beyond. Soon, as if a supercharged sports car had overtaken a farm
tractor, the Victor tanker was far behind me.

Back on the ground at Leuchars, I had issues to ponder. As I contemplated my problematic descent, I thought of the individual, or individuals,
who had decided not to equip the Lightning with a radio altimeter. This
instrument would have resolved, in an instant, the predicament of descent
in borderline cloud conditions. No doubt the installation process would
have been costly, but rather less costly than the loss of an aircraft and its
expensively-trained pilot. I thought about the period before I initiated the

descent and how my rough calculations had worked out. I felt pleased about that – although in truth I knew that luck had been on my side. This, of course, was just as well since, if a game of Russian roulette was involved (or any other form of gambling game for that matter), then luck would be a key element. When I pondered this and how my recent activity had been performed in the cause of the defence of my country, I realised that the flight had been a necessary part of a much larger picture. And that, surely, should not be treated as a game where life or death activities are decided as if by the flick of a coin.

Chapter 13

A MAN'S
AIRCRAFT

*ALAN WHITE
RECOLLECTS*

I came relatively late to the Lightning. I had flown the Hawker Hunter in the air defence and ground attack roles and, while in Singapore for the latter, I saw a film clip of Lightnings performing at Farnborough The clip, taken in the early 1960s, showed take-off rotations into near-vertical climbs. I was instantly enthralled. I had to fly that aircraft.

My chance came some seven years later when I was appointed as a flight commander on 11 (F) Squadron at RAF Leuchars, Scotland. By then I was so familiar with the Hunter that it was almost as if I could make the machine talk to me. Surely it would be the same for the Lightning – or so I thought until one of the instructors at the conversion unit at RAF Coltishall asked me, perhaps tongue-in-cheek, whether I would be: "one of the few squadron leaders we let through this course." I soon discovered that the record of failures at Coltishall among potential Lightning flight commanders was, indeed, high.

Despite this, I passed the course although shortly after arriving at Leuchars I blotted my copy-book on my first air-to-air refuelling flight. The flight ended in failure when, instead of using the tanker as a formation reference point, I focussed on the basket itself. This was a cardinal error especially in turbulent flight conditions. I did not make that error again which was just as well for, within a few months of my joining the squadron, our pilots' in-flight refuelling abilities were well-tested on a trip to RAF Tengah in Singapore. This flight, a marathon for short-range fighters, was designed to prove the ability of the Lightning Force to reinforce the Far East at speed and with minimum stops en-route. I was scheduled to lead a pair of aircraft out of Leuchars at 0140, an unsociable time dictated by our group headquarters' desire to make the trip as testing as possible.

The date was January 1969 and as I and my number two walked out to our aircraft the air was crisply cold, a light dusting of snow swirled across the ground and the star-speckled sky seemed sublimely clear. We performed walk-around checks then clambered into our cockpits. My own cockpit was a clutter of maps, booklets of flight and airfield data, a packet of absurdly neat bite-sized sandwiches designed to be popped into the mouth during brief removals of the oxygen mask, a pint-sized Tupperware container of orange juice plus straw, and a so-called 'piddle-pack' (an important item for the eight-hour first leg to Bahrain, assuming one could overcome the problem of using it as we were well trussed-up in our immersion suits for the first leg). Overnight stops were planned at Muharraq on Bahrain Island and at RAF Gan in the Maldives.

Over Cambridge, my number two and I rendezvoused with our first Victor tanker. The Victor topped us up with fuel straightaway then transferred fuel to a second tanker destined to be with us as far as Malta. In fact we were accompanied by Victor tankers for the whole flight to Singapore, flying in close or loose formation with them depending on cloud conditions. From time to time we exchanged each of these mother hens for others at pre-planned rendezvous points. As few countries allowed flight-refuelling over their territory, and others were simply hostile to foreign military aircraft, our route was far from direct. The first leg took us over France (with a strict embargo on flight-refuelling) to Nice in the south of France, off the west coast of Italy (skirting Corsica and Sardinia) to overhead Malta. Then on to Cyprus, along the CENTO (Central Treaty Organisation) route north from Cyprus to Ankara, due east to Tehran, then south from Tehran to Bahrain. The final leg jinked around the northern tip of Sumatra, down the Mallaca Straits to Singapore. The planning requirements for a Lightning squadron deployment to Singapore, and the costs, were illustrated by the figures for our trip: a total of 228 in-flight refuelling contacts and some 400 air and ground crew – mainly Victor personnel – pre-deployed at various points along the route.

By flying accompanied, the Lightnings enjoyed the benefits of the Victors' long-range radio communications kit as well as their superior navigational equipment. However there were penalties. The transit speed chosen for the Victors, 0.8 Mach, was on the slow side for the Lightnings and the consequent slight loss of effectiveness of flight controls and engine response at our heights and weights (with over-wing and internal fuel tanks topped-up to high levels) made close formation flying hard work for any length of time. One time, for instance, my number two and I flew below and behind our tanker's wing in dense, turbulent cloud for two hours on the Gan to Tengah leg. Moreover, on that leg our tanker captain took us up to 47,000 feet as he sought smooth flight conditions to enable us to get our refuelling probes into the Victor's wildly swinging baskets. When we had made contact at that height, the only way to keep the probes of our wallowing beasts in the baskets was to bang-in the Lightnings' reheats every time we began to slide back.

There were sections of the trip when we were quite definitely pushing our luck. On the leg to Gan, for example, and again on the leg from Gan to Tengah, there were parts when we were beyond any possible diversion unless our fuel tanks were full. As a result, and to guard against failure to obtain fuel, we had to enter those stretches plugged-in, and remain plugged-in, essentially burning fuel directly from the mother-hen's tanks.

Arriving at Gan, and eager to get on the ground after almost five hours in the cramped confines of the Lightning's cockpit, I looked forward to a good stretch and a cool, refreshing beer. However, suddenly I faced a mini-drama when, as I selected the undercarriage down, the starboard main wheel failed to respond. Normally, a reassuring clunk would be heard as the wheels locked in the down position, reinforcing the 'three greens' displayed on the cockpit indicator. When I heard only one main wheel clunk, I knew without even having to check the indicator that one of the main wheel lights would show red. The advice in the emergency flip cards for such an occurrence was unambiguous: a landing should not be attempted as the aircraft was likely to cartwheel.

While my number two landed, I flew low and slow past the air traffic control tower for a visual check. The controller confirmed that the starboard leg was out of its housing, but by no more than a few inches. I made a couple of further selections of undercarriage up and down, though the situation did not change. I thought of trying the undercarriage emergency air bottle (charged to 1,000 psi) even though there was nothing wrong, seemingly, with the main hydraulic system (charged to 3,000 psi). I decided to defy logic and try anyway...but without success. The only – and, I felt, not entirely useful – advice from the laconic Lightning pilot pre-positioned in Gan's air traffic control tower was: "eject over the lagoon, there are fewer sharks there."

At this point I decided to ignore the 250 knot speed limit for flying with the undercarriage selected down. I therefore pointed towards the sea and accelerated to 500 knots. At that airspeed I kicked on a boot-full of rudder to skid the aircraft away from the recalcitrant wheel, an action which, to my great relief, did the trick. The force of the 500 knot airflow caught the few inches of lowered wheel, and blasted down the leg without apparent damage to itself or to the other undercarriage legs, or even to the two overwing tanks. After another slow pass over the air traffic control tower to confirm my belief that all was well, I landed, albeit gingerly, and came to a safe stop on the runway. I was met by members of the squadron ground crew with a tractor, a towing-arm, undercarriage leg-clamps – and the all important ice-cold beer. The belated beer tasted all the better and I was more than happy to have avoided a swim in the lagoon.

As a postscript to all of this, the aircraft was ground tested at Gan and, as is so often the case in the flying business, no fault was found. Mounted on a test rig the undercarriage repeatedly raised and lowered without the slightest hesitation. I took the engineers' assurances on trust and with no (serious) reservations climbed into my aircraft the next day and took off for Tengah. There, when I selected the undercarriage down for landing, it worked perfectly.

The incident reminded me of another example of 'no fault found' when an 11 Squadron pilot reported a flight control restriction. No-one likes an unsolved fault, still less the implication that an airborne problem has been imagined. In this case, though, the control restriction re-occurred two flights later. This time, with both engines removed to facilitate a thorough check of the control runs, the source of the problem was revealed: a wooden broom handle had been left inside the fuselage, possibly during manufacture of the aircraft, and eventually had shifted into a position where it interfered with the freedom of control movement.

It was interesting to be back in Singapore six years after I had left at the end of my tour on Hawker Hunter aircraft there – and in a totally different aeroplane. In the Hunter we were blind in the cloudy conditions that often prevailed at height, and most certainly we were not aware of embedded and deadly thunder clouds until we blundered into them. Now, in the Lightning with its airborne intercept radar, we could find high-level targets, map the coastline and, best of all, spot the hard centres of storm clouds.

When the station commander from Leuchars came to visit the squadron we took the group captain downtown to sample Singapore's nightlife. All seemed to go well until it was time to return to Tengah at which point we were surrounded by a group of light-fingered, sarong-wearing girls who importuned and offered 'services'. I suddenly realised, as I was scrambling into one of our two cars, that a fairly substantial sum of money that I had stashed into my hip pocket had gone. I climbed out of the car and searched the sea of faces for the girl who had momentarily distracted my attention by caressing my crotch. I recognised her and grabbed her. The group captain then climbed out of the car and came to my aid shouting: "Hold her and I'll get the police!" This sparked a wail of entreaties from the other girls: "No, no! No police!" I shook the girl I had grabbed and saw some money emerge at her feet from beneath the sarong. I shook again, and continued to shake her until I reckoned about the right amount had reached the ground, whereupon I picked up the money and we beat a hasty retreat back to Tengah and the relative (and air-conditioned) tranquillity of the officers' mess bar.

There were no dramas on the way home from Singapore, at least not for the Lightnings. However the Victor tanker that I and my number two had picked up overhead Malta, and which was planned to accompany us as far as East Anglia, suddenly went into a dive as we approached overhead Nice. I thought something catastrophic must have occurred and started to follow the Victor down. I pressed my radio transmit button and asked about the problem but got no answer until the Victor had levelled out some 30,000 feet below our original height. At this stage a rather shaky voice answered my call to explain that they had suffered a major electrical system failure and that they would divert to the French air force base at Orange. As we had recently topped-up with fuel and as there was nothing we could do to assist, I told the Victor captain that we would continue unaccompanied. I asked him to radio the tanker cell at RAF Marham to pass on this information and to tell them that we would rendezvous with the next tanker, as per schedule, as we approached the English coast. Somehow the message got distorted and we were a little surprised and disturbed to meet two 'rescue' Victors that hastened towards us, refuelling hoses trailed, over Paris. This, as might be imagined, created something of a diplomatic storm.

Back at Leuchars we settled down to normal squadron training in addition to the QRA commitment which gave ample opportunities to chase Soviet aircraft in the northern reaches of the UK air defence region. As time passed, and as I became increasingly familiar with all aspects of the Lightning's role and superlative performance, I derived unceasing pleasure from flying the machine. The Lightning was a thoroughbred in which a pilot could readily 'slip the surly bonds of earth'. As a working military machine, however, the aircraft could be considered less than perfect in a number of respects, for example the small load of just two missiles compared to the F4 Phantom's eight, and the performance of the airborne radar which was near abysmal at low level. On a dark night the concentration required to pick up and pursue a low-flying target meant that it was all too easy to drop dangerously low. It's a fair bet that there are few Lightning pilots who have not given themselves a fright on glancing from the radar picture to the aircraft instruments for a quick check only to find the altimeter reading very close to zero.

This particular risk was brought home to me in a tragic way shortly after my tour on 11 Squadron ended and I had moved to RAF Binbrook to take command of 5 Squadron. A NATO team had descended on the station without warning, as was standard practice, and had declared us to be at 'war'. This was the annual tactical evaluation. 5 Squadron's US exchange pilot, Captain Bill Schaffner USAF, who was relatively new and eager to shine, was brought to cockpit readiness as darkness fell. After an hour in the cockpit he was ordered airborne but the order was cancelled before he reached the take-off point. He returned to dispersal, asked for a fuel top-up but, before full engineering turn-round procedures could be completed, was scrambled again. He started engines in a rush and began to move, very obviously anxious to waste no time. He was handed over to ground radar at Patrington as he reached 10,000 feet and instructed to accelerate to 0.95 Mach (around 600 knots). He was then told to descend in order to intercept and shadow a low-level target that was, at that stage, twenty-eight miles from his position. He was not told that the target's airspeed was a mere 160 knots.

He was directed by Patrington and was heard to call 'contact' when he had picked up the target on his airborne radar. This would have been at a range of less than five to seven miles distance. A moment or two later he said that he had to "manoeuvre to lose speed". Shortly after this call the crew of the target, a Shackleton aircraft, reported that the Lightning's lights had gone out. The Lightning had hit the sea about 200 yards behind the Shackleton.

I was strapping into a Lightning to come to cockpit alert when Binbrook's station commander climbed up my aircraft's ladder and beckoned me to climb out. He told me briefly what had happened and that, while an immediate air and sea search had been mounted, he was not at all optimistic about the possibility of Bill's survival. I drove to my married quarter, picked up Esmé, my wife, and went round to Bill's married quarter to be with Bill's wife, Linda. We sat with her throughout that night and most of the following day until some friends arrived from the USAF base at Alconbury. Linda remained totally convinced, long after the search was called off and long after she had been repatriated to the United States, that Bill was alive and would be found.

The wreckage of Bill's Lightning was located without difficulty, but two months elapsed before it was raised from the seabed. The cockpit was found to be empty. When this was revealed by the Humberside press, local UFO enthusiasts linked the incident to alleged sightings of bright lights and spacecraft and claimed that Bill had been abducted by aliens. Soon, the national press expanded the story and even the BBC broadcast a rather silly programme that aired a variety of loony opinions. All of this could have been laughed off except for the fact that it added quite unnecessarily to Linda's distress. The sad truth was that Bill Schaffner had fallen foul of the dangers of low-level work in the dark.

That incident proved to be the low point of my time in command of 5 Squadron. For the high point, I would probably choose the squadron's success in the 1971 AFCENT (Allied Forces Central Europe) air defence competition. We started to prepare for this early in the year, practising the subsonic and supersonic interception profiles we had been told to expect. We selected our six best pilots and identified the most reliable of the squadron's radar modules. We ensured that these modules, along with the specific Lightnings that would carry them, were in peak condition by early April when we were due to compete.

The rules of the competition required that a nominated pair of aircraft were airborne within four minutes of the order to scramble. A second pair was allowed to start engines and to act as substitutes – at a penalty – should either or both of the first pair fail to go. Pilots were required to be out of, and not touching, their aircraft prior to the scramble order. We practised quick-start procedures endlessly from January onwards, shinning up the cockpit ladder before we leapt into the cockpit, used the left hand to plug in the common connector for oxygen, communications lead and anti-g suit while, simultaneously, the right hand pressed the start button for number one engine. This was followed by the number two start button the instant the first engine began to wind up. Connection of ejection seat straps and leg restraints followed immediately, while eyes monitored the engine instruments to check that all warning lights were out. A member of ground crew then removed and stowed the top ejection seat safety pins before he slid down and took away the cockpit ladder. Closing the cockpit canopy was a signal from pilot to ground crew to remove the wheel chocks. All of our six chosen pilots could get airborne within two minutes of the order to scramble, a speed that so surprised the AFCENT judges that one judge was nominated to climb up the ladder after a pilot to check that he was strapping in properly.

We had calculated that to beat our competitors, especially the USAF F4 Phantoms stationed on the Continent, we would have to complete all interceptions within 125 seconds of the target crossing the start line. We were well short of this, though, almost up to the start of the competition. However, for the competition itself our pairs came first and second on the day subsonic event, first and second on the day supersonic event, and first and third on the night subsonic event. These results plus the high serviceability of our aircraft, combined with our filmed record of missile 'firings' within precise range and angle-off criteria, clinched the competition for us.

A month after the competition and the subsequent celebrations, the squadron lost another aircraft. Ali McKay, one of the AFCENT competitors, took off for a night sortie in an aircraft that had just returned from deep servicing at a specialised maintenance unit. About ninety seconds after take-off he had an indication of fire in the number one engine, followed almost immediately by warnings of fire in the reheat areas of both engines. He declared an emergency, headed for the coast and climbed to a safe ejection altitude of 10,000 feet. His number two, who had taken off a minute or so after him, reported a brilliant white flame from the rear of Ali's Lightning. By now Ali had lost elevator control and had no option, therefore, but to abandon his aircraft. As he descended in his parachute towards the sea he carried out all the briefed and rehearsed procedures in copybook fashion. He was rescued from the water in commendably quick time by a helicopter from RAF Leconfield.

Without wishing to detract from Ali's contribution to his own survival, I believe the dry-runs that were part of every squadron's training schedule helped to ensure that the correct reactions came more readily *in extremis*. Remembering the sad loss of a pilot on 11 Squadron who, after a successful ejection in similar circumstances, screwed completely his chances of survival through a catalogue of errors, I was determined that everyone on 5 Squadron should take survival drills seriously. I insisted that our aircrew dived into Binbrook's open-air swimming pool in winter in their immersion-suits to experience how quickly hands became uselessly numb in icy-cold water. Probably, this would not have helped Bill Schaffner, nonetheless I was determined to try to improve the odds for anyone flying an aircraft that, at the time, had a propensity to catch fire.

A couple of months after Ali's bale-out the squadron was detached to Akrotiri, Cyprus, to practise firing the guns that had recently been added to the Lightning's weapon capability. Detachments to Cyprus were always popular and we counted ourselves lucky to go twice during the two years that I was in command. We took eleven aircraft for both detachments, in-flight refuelling to Cyprus in one hop, and again in one hop for the return to UK.

Our first visit to Akrotiri happened to coincide with the officers' mess summer ball. After two weeks of determined effort on the firing range by day, and a few night sorties to take advantage of the region's relatively early onset of darkness, we all looked forward to the summer ball. During the ball itself, however, one of our pilots, a little the worse due to a few glasses of Cypriot wine, decided it would be a good joke to move and hide the station commander's car. In doing so, he inadvertently ran over some glass and punctured a tyre. When the station commander, an air commodore renowned for his short temper, eventually found his car he was not at all pleased – incandescent in fact. The following day he tasked his second-in-

Top left: Four Mk 1As of 56(F) Squadron break into the circuit at RAF Wattisham.

Top right: Line of Lightning Mk 1As of 56(F) Squadron in Firebird colour scheme, RAF Wattisham.

Above left: Pilot dismounting from 56(F) Squadron two-seater Lightning T4 at RAF Wattisham.

Above right: 111(F) Squadron Mk 3 Lightning at RAF Wattisham.

Top left: 56(F) Squadron Mk 3 closing in on the basket of a Victor tanker above Mount Etna, Sicily.

Top right: 56(F) Squadron Mk 3 with two Victor tankers as company.

Above: View from the right-hand side of Lightning T5 XS456. Picture taken by Graham Perry on 18th September 1974. This was his first Lightning sortie soon after appointment as senior engineering officer (SEngO) of 11 Squadron.

Left: 56(F) Squadron Lightning Mk 3s flying in echelon port formation. The aircraft sport the infamous chequer board fin markings.

Top: In this picture, taken by Roger Colebrook, the tanker is in a left turn as the Lightning T5 closes in on the right-hand hose. Roger was in the right seat undergoing his familiarisation with in-flight refuelling procedures, Akrotiri, 1967.

Middle: Roger Colebrook astern the drogue in 56 Squadron Lightning T5, 1967.

Bottom: Three pilots of 56(F) Squadron (Roger Colebrook on left) walk out to their aircraft at Akrotiri, Cyprus.

Top left: Roger Colebrook in aircrew wet dinghy drill in Cyprus.

Top right: View from 19 Squadron hangar at Gütersloh, Germany, 1969.

Above: 56(F) Squadron Lightning Mk 6 on the approach to landing.

Left: Visiting Danish F104 pilots with 19(F) Squadron pilots, RAF Gütersloh, 1969. RAF pilots *L-R:* Bob Turbin, Laurie Jones (CO), Peter Naz, Roger Beazley, Phil Williamson, Richard Pike.

Left: Flight Lieutenant P W Roser and Flying Officer J W Cliffe with their 11 Squadron Mk 6s practising air-to-air refuelling on the new (1974-1975) Victor K2. (UK MOD Crown Copyright 1974)

Middle: 92 Squadron Mk 2A at RAF Gütersloh, 1975.

Below: Cockpit of the Lightning forerunner, English Electric P1.

Top: Line of 11 Squadron Lightning tails at RAF Binbrook.

Above left: 56 Squadron (the Firebirds) Mk 1A, 1963 (photo via Dick Cloke).

Above right: XR725, the 23 Squadron Mk 6 which Squadron Leader Ed Durham flew to Canada in 1968.

Left: 74 Squadron's XS897. Pilot Flt Lt Roger Pope is somewhere over Iran on the way back to the UK from Singapore (taken by Dave Roome).

Top and above: These pictures show the difference between the 'new' air defence grey camouflage of 1982, and the 'old' disruptive camouflage dating from 1975-76. The shade of grey finally chosen was known as 'Barley Grey' after the project scientist at Farnborough. The colour is used by many air forces to this day.

Left: Fg Off K G Carvosso conducts pre-flight inspection of his Lightning Mk 6 at RAF Binbrook.

Top: Aircrew and ground crew of 11(F) Squadron stand by their Lightnings for formal inspection by the Duchess of Gloucester, 1975. Wg Cdr Ted Nance RAF, the squadron commander, is on the left, in front of the whole squadron. Officers nearest the camera are the two flight commanders, Sqn Ldr Harry Drew AFC RAF, and Sqn Ldr Norman Barker RAF.

Middle: A rehearsal of the line-up of aircraft for the Duchess of Gloucester's visit to RAF Binbrook, early 1975.

Bottom: Lightning Training Flight T5 firing a Firestreak air-to-air missile.

command, a group captain, to make enquiries. The group captain came to see me to ask if I knew anything about the incident. I had not, until about an hour beforehand when a somewhat shame-faced pilot had turned up to confess all and to ask what he should do. I suggested that he ought to apologise to the station commander but added that there might be some danger as the man was known for his wrath. The miscreant decided, therefore, against this, and I confess I could not disagree with this decision. However, I then had to try to persuade the group captain, without actually lying to him, that it was highly unlikely that any member of 5 Squadron was involved. A couple of days later, during an exercise called by the station commander, several of 5 Squadron's officers and most of our airmen were tasked to mount guard for twenty-four hours in some very unlikely and very unpleasant locations. I had to assume that suspicion had fallen on us.

Back at Binbrook once more, we concentrated on our night flying commitment. Half of the Lightning squadrons' annual task involved night flying and 5 Squadron had lost a lot of dark time in the early part of the year as we prepared for the AFCENT competition. Flying night after night in the Lightning was not everyone's idea of fun, not least, perhaps, because landing on an ill-lit runway at around 200 miles per hour could seem more akin to a controlled crash than a finely-judged touchdown. Some compensation, though, came in the form of the much-enjoyed night flying supper – eggs, bacon, tomatoes, and beans. Accompanied by a pint or two of best bitter beer, this helped us to wind down after two, three or even four adrenaline-charged trips.

For some, however, this wind-down session was not enough. One time, when I was on 11 Squadron, a member of my flight had asked to speak with me privately. He was about to walk out for a night flying exercise and confessed that he simply could not do it; he could not face going up at night again. Another pilot, a very experienced Lightning man, got as far as the take-off point but found he could not bring himself to open up the throttles. He had to taxi back, almost on the point of breaking down. For another young first-tour pilot on 11 Squadron, the dark alone was not the problem. He experienced what seemed to be a panic attack during a daytime flight. He called out to his formation leader that he could not distinguish up from down. It was only when the leader closed on him and thus provided a point of reference that it proved possible to lead the young pilot down and back for a landing.

I'm sure that all who fly experience some degree of apprehension before take-off – surely an essential ingredient for self-preservation. However, I cannot recall the same level of stress on other fighter types as that generated in the Lightning world. During my conversion course, the chief flying instructor had introduced us to the Lightning on our first day with the comment: "this is a man's aircraft; it is not for the boys." I thought this sounded a little over-dramatic at the time, but perhaps he was not too far off the mark. Fortunately, there were men who were willing to take on the Lightning and its role and enjoy both.

Chapter 14

TWENTY LIGHTNING YEARS

PETER COLLINS LOOKS BACK ON A LONG ASSOCIATION WITH THE LIGHTNING

The English Electric Lightning dominated twenty years of my flying experience in the Royal Air Force. I helped to introduce the aircraft into Fighter Command, wrote pilots' notes for the aircraft, served as a flight commander on 23(F) and 11(F) Squadrons, commanded 111(F) Squadron and then, as station commander at RAF Gütersloh, had 19(F) and 92(F) Squadrons under command in Germany at the height of the Cold War.

Leading up to those days, I had been involved in the fighter pilot world for some years. After two operational tours in the 1950s, I had been posted as a trials pilot to the All-Weather Development Squadron of the Central Fighter Establishment at RAF West Raynham. At that time, the Central Fighter Establishment was the storehouse of fighter expertise where budding Douglas Baders and 'Cats' Eyes' Cunninghams honed their skills in the Day Fighter Leaders' School or the All-Weather Fighter Combat School. New fighter aircraft, tactics and weapons were evaluated in the two development squadrons – the aforementioned All-Weather Development Squadron and the Air Fighting Development Squadron.

Ten years earlier such a prospect for me would have seemed improbable, to say the least. That is not to say that I lacked a service background. In 1919 my father had joined the newly-formed Royal Air Force as a wireless operator. After his training, he had spent eight years flying in De Havilland DH9As and Bristol Fighters over the inhospitable territory of the North West Frontier. He had left the service in 1927 but was recalled from civilian life in 1939. In World War Two he rose to the rank of squadron leader and ended up with an Order of the British Empire and three Mentions in Despatches. My father was instrumental in arranging my first ever flight which took place in August 1945 when I was an unofficial passenger in a B17 Flying Fortress. However, I was fifteen years old at the time and although I enjoyed the flight, I don't believe it inspired any latent desire to make the Royal Air Force my career.

In spite of this, when I arrived at Birmingham University three years later to read history, I was attracted to join the University Air Squadron. I have to admit that I was tempted more by the £35 a year bounty than by the enticement to learn to fly. However, learn to fly I did and I flew my first solo in August 1949 in a De Havilland Tiger Moth aircraft. Two years after that, on graduation from Birmingham University, I was called up into the RAF for National Service. My status in the Royal Air Force Volunteer Reserve as a university officer cadet allowed me to start as an acting pilot officer (on probation) and to avoid the square-bashing at Padgate, Warrington which was the normal lot for conscripts. I went straight on to the advanced flying training course at Syerston near Newark-on-Trent to fly the unforgiving piston-engined Harvard aircraft.

The Korean War was in progress and, as the RAF was expanding to meet operational demands, no time was wasted during our training. Six months after I had joined the service I was sent to Driffield, East Yorkshire for conversion onto Gloster Meteor jet aircraft. In less than a year from enlistment I was posted to my first operational tour, flying Meteor 8s on 63 Squadron at Waterbeach, near Cambridge. The excitement and job satisfaction I found there persuaded me to apply for a short service commission which I was awarded in 1954. From single-seat day fighters I then moved to two-seat all-weather operations on Venom 3 night-fighters and Gloster Javelin aircraft, completing a second tour during which I was appointed a permanent commission. After this, I was posted to the All-Weather Development Squadron in April 1958. For eighteen months I was involved in various trials on the Javelin, often carrying the newly-introduced Firestreak guided air-to-air missile. We learnt then that the Lightning, the RAF's first single-seat, radar-equipped all-weather supersonic fighter, would be coming to the Central Fighter Establishment for evaluation. In 1959 the two development squadrons were merged into a single squadron commanded by Wing Commander Jimmy Dell who had spent the last two years as the Fighter Command liaison officer with the English Electric Company.

A team of four was selected to conduct the Lightning trials with Jimmy Dell. I was fortunate to be one of those selected (probably because I had experience of both day fighter and all-weather roles). We began to prepare for the arrival of the first Lightning, although no service simulator was available at that stage and there was no sign of a two-seat version (the first LightningT4 trainer did not arrive until mid-1962). We had access to a prototype simulator, developed by a company in Aylesbury, but this proved to be super-sensitive and, if anything, tended to dishearten us although we gained some familiarity with cockpit layout and cockpit checks. In case anything should go wrong on the initial sorties, we planned to use a Hawker Hunter as a chase aircraft flown by a member of the trials team. As the only non-Hunter qualified member of the team, I had to convert quickly to type. We did not have time for the extensive ground school and dual instruction needed nowadays so, after a couple of flights with our qualified flying instructor in the two-seat Hunter T7, I was sent off solo in a single-seat Hunter Mark 6.

A few days before Christmas 1959, Lightning XG334 was flown from Warton to our base at Coltishall, Norfolk. The silver, supersonic icon had arrived and it gleamed. At fifty-five feet long and, at the tip of the tailplane, some twenty feet high, the aircraft appeared huge – especially when parked next to the Hawker Hunter. The deep, slab-sided appearance with one engine mounted above the other meant that, unlike the Gloster Meteor, there would not be asymmetric problems if one engine should fail. Over the next few days the four of us experienced our first Lightning flights. For us all, the event was awesome. One team member said that everything happened so fast that he was tempted to log the flight as passenger time! My turn finally came on New Year's Eve, 1959.

As I climbed the ladder to the tiny cockpit my sense of excitement seemed to mount with each step. I strapped-in, went through the by-now well-memorised pre-start checks then signalled 'engine start' to the attendant ground crew. When I pressed the number one engine start button, a high-pitched squeal from the Avpin starter was followed by a whoosh as the engine sprang to life. Soon, with both engines turning and burning, I began to taxi out for take-off. I found that using a brake handle on the control column, as most RAF fighters employed, was a considerable improvement on the Javelin's toe-brake arrangement which could cause problems. On the runway, I applied the brakes as I ran both engines up to 90% power. When satisfied with jet pipe temperature and other readings, I released the brakes, pushed both throttles forward to the 100% cold power position and immediately experienced the legendary kick-in-the-back from the unleashed power of two Rolls-Royce Avon engines.

The chase Hawker Hunter, airborne some fifteen minutes ahead of me, was at an altitude of around 8,000 feet over Coltishall airfield as it waited to observe my flight. I glimpsed the Hunter as I powered up like a rocket, but within seconds it was left far behind. When I approached an altitude of 36,000 feet I began to ease off the power before I started to explore the Lightning's handling characteristics. I found the controls well-balanced and responsive and I was impressed by the rate of roll. In high-g turns (although I limited myself to 3 g at this early stage) I was impressed, also, to discover that subsonic airspeeds could be maintained by use of cold engine power alone, without reheat. As the flight progressed I felt that, in aerodynamic terms at least, this would prove to be a most effective fighter. Before long, as my fuel state dictated the need to return to Coltishall, I initiated descent and set up for a visual circuit at the airfield. I flew a fairly wide downwind leg, lowered the undercarriage and flaps as part of the pre-landing checks, and stabilised the airspeed at 175 knots on finals. As the airfield boundary approached, I eased the airspeed back to 155 knots before I made a positive touchdown on the runway.

As I taxied the Lightning back to dispersal, my sense of elation was buoyant indeed. Challenges, though, lay ahead, the chief of which was how best to use the aircraft's airborne interception radar. Unlike previous Royal Air Force aircraft with a navigator to interpret the radar, the Lightning pilot would have to do it all. The Lightning's radar system, designated AI 23 by the RAF, was called 'Airpass' by the manufacturers, the Ferranti Company, (airborne interception radar and pilot attack sight system).

Ferranti's brochure claimed that the pilot would acquire his target on radar, lock on to it then transfer his attention to the head-up pilot attack sight where he would see an aiming dot and a tracking circle. The reality, unfortunately, was not so straightforward. AI lock-on could be detected by Soviet bombers with radar warning devices and electronic jamming equipment, and the Lightning's missile, just the Firestreak in those early days, was a stern attack weapon which needed to see the target's hot jet pipes. If the Lightning intercepted a head-on target (the most likely scenario in an air defence situation), 'flying the dot' would merely lead to a collision course from which the Firesteak could never acquire lock-on.

The only way around this problem was to keep the AI in search mode. The Lightning pilot, therefore, would have to interpret his radar picture and plan a path for a stern attack. His workload would be considerable. He would have to view his small radar screen through an extended rubber visor, operate the radar controls with his left hand and continue to fly the aircraft with his right hand. Meanwhile, he would have to employ mental mathematics to work out a target's heading and height, with the limited information on his radar screen, before he planned an attack path.

In the course of the trials we assessed a range of interception profiles: subsonic and supersonic; day and night; high and low level. One night, I was tasked to carry out low level interception profiles. The night was clear and starlit. As I headed out to sea and as I crossed the Norfolk coast, I noted that large numbers of fishing boat lights were spread across the surface of the water. At 500 feet above the sea, with my face pressed against the radar visor, I concentrated on trying to pick out my target. The AI 23 was poor at low level but eventually I spotted the target and began to manoeuvre towards a stern attack position. During the turn, as I glanced outside the cockpit, I was appalled to see the stars below me, and the fishing boats above. The world had suddenly inverted itself. With my heart thumping, I focussed on regaining control of the aircraft in straight and level flight. After this experience, it was decided to raise the minimum height for night interceptions from 500 feet to 1,000 feet.

In March 1960, not long into the trials, we lost our first aircraft, XG334. The pilot, Ron Harding, tried to lower the Lightning's undercarriage but the port leg became stuck in a partially-down position. Despite all of his efforts, Ron Harding was unable to lower the undercarriage and our instructions in such an event were clear: landing was not to be attempted. He therefore climbed to 15,000 feet, pointed the Lightning out to sea, and pulled his ejection seat handle. Unfortunately, the seat failed to stabilise during the ejection sequence, it tumbled and entered a flat spin. Ron, though, kept a cool head and, despite severe disorientation, managed to disentangle some parachute shroud lines from his legs before he belatedly separated from the seat to make a safe parachute landing.

Some months later, after a successful night supersonic sortie, I commenced descent for my return to base. However, when I selected the airbrake switch in the descent, the airbrakes failed to operate. As the Lightning's hydraulic pressure seemed normal, I was not unduly bothered and continued the descent, fairly low on fuel after the supersonic work. When I selected the undercarriage down at the appropriate moment, the port leg unlocked but the starboard leg and the nose-wheel failed to lower. In the Coltishall circuit area I made further undercarriage selections, to no avail. I operated the emergency undercarriage system, after which my cockpit indicator, instead of the necessary 'three greens', showed the nose-wheel locked down and both of the main wheels unlocked.

Matters now looked bad, especially as my fuel state was seriously low. Normally we were required to land with 400lbs of fuel reserves in each of the main tanks, but I was already below that amount. To conserve a little fuel, I shut down the number two engine and transferred all of the remaining fuel to the number one engine. I tried to shake the wheels down with positive 'g' and I performed some violent manoeuvres in yaw, pitch and roll, but all to no effect. Now resigned to ejection, I climbed reluctantly back up to 10,000 feet, selected a safe heading and tightened my seat straps in anticipation of the bale out. I was poised to pull the ejection seat handle when suddenly I noticed the port main wheel lock down. This was auspicious indeed and I felt encouraged to turn back towards base, even if more in hope than expectation. However during the turn the starboard red light also changed to green. Providence, it seemed, had intervened but only just in time!

By this stage, though, the Lightning was dangerously low on fuel. I still had to decide whether to eject or whether to continue. If the engine stopped my hydraulically-powered flight controls would seize, but I resolved to shut my mind to this possibility and to press on with a ground radar-monitored approach. My ejection seat would still be effective, even at ground level, but I was conscious of the possibility of casualties on the ground in the event of a last-minute ejection. Fortunately, my luck held and I landed safely, though when I shut-down the aircraft at the far end of the runway my fuel state registered 25lbs on number one engine, and zero on number two. A sortie that normally would have lasted forty-five minutes had extended to seventy minutes. Shortly after this episode, the authorities raised the minimum fuel requirement at landing from 400lbs to 800lbs a side.

The All-Weather Development Squadron had an annual liaison visit with its French opposite number, the military experimental centre at Mont-de-Marsan. I went there on two occasions, both times to fly the Super Mystère and the Mirage 3. The Super Mystère was closely modelled on the American F100 Super Sabre, while the Mirage 3 was more comparable with the Lightning. Both the Mystère and the Mirage 3 were single-seat fighters and, as was normal then, we flew them with a minimum of fuss and preparation. Pilot's notes, in French of course, were perused swiftly, after which we received a quick talk from an English-speaking capitaine, a cockpit brief followed by (in a heavy French accent): "off you go, no sweat!" I was impressed by the Mirage 3 in particular. This aircraft was as speedy as the Lightning, and I felt had a better cockpit layout, but the radar (Cyrano by Thomson-CSF) was inferior to the Lightning's AI 23 in my opinion.

I became involved, too, in a lecture tour to South Africa and Southern Rhodesia (as Zimbabwe was known in those days). The tour was led by our commandant Hughie Edwards VC DSO DFC, a jovial Australian who was not overly endowed with tact. At a late-night celebration which developed into a sing-song he launched into the notorious Boer War marching song...*See – the boys in blue are marching and I can no longer stay...Hark – I hear the bugle calling, goodbye Dolly Gray*. This was performed in the face of a crowd of well-lubricated South Africans who fortunately took it well.

Towards the end of 1961 I was posted away from Coltishall to the Royal Air Force Handling Squadron at Boscombe Down. By the mid-1970s, when I was at RAF Gütersloh, I had flown every mark of Lightning apart from the Saudi version. In my opinion the Lightning Mark 2A was the best version of the aircraft.

Of the number of different aircraft types that I flew during my service career, the English Electric Lightning was, for me, the finest. By the time of its retirement from the RAF, the Lightning had completed twenty-eight years of frontline service. I feel privileged to have been involved with this iconic aircraft for all but eight of those years.

Chapter 15

SUPERSONIC
STRETCH

John Hall, left, was at the end of his second Lightning tour when his double flame-out occurred. After Gütersloh he instructed on Hunters at Brawdy, where this photo was taken.

JOHN HALL PUSHES THE BOUNDARIES

The atmosphere, bizarrely, was a mix of merriment and tension. The duty operations officer stared at me, his expression quizzical: "Are you quite sure about that?" he said.

The hour was getting late, the dark December night of 1976 had an ominous air. The night flying programme had been completed and we were keen to retire to the officers' mess for a jar or two of Warsteiner beer and a chat. After all, quite apart from the immediate issue, there was rather a lot that we needed to talk about. There was, for instance, the small matter of the squadron's impending metamorphosis: in a month or so, our 19(F) Squadron's Lightning Mk 2As were due to be ousted and replaced by F4 Phantom aircraft. The squadron would reform at Wildenrath, a base far from our current home of Gütersloh in West Germany's northern reaches. And we Lightning pilots along with our ground crews and other personnel would be unceremoniously dispersed. With Gütersloh just seventy or so miles from the border with East Germany, we had been at the sharp end of NATO's air defence for years. Now all of that was about to change – a change, in our opinion, that had distinctly retrograde prospects.

Take, for one thing, the Battle Flight commitment. This quick reaction alert system had meant two Lightnings on constant readiness to be airborne within five minutes. By any standards, that was fast – faster than the time required in the UK (normally ten minutes) and faster, we felt sure, than could be achieved in the two-crew F4. That was another thing: the two-crew issue. As Lightning pilots we had been taught self-sufficiency. There was no-one else on board to hold our hands. Some of us had received posting notices to re-train on the F4 and we knew this would mean a whole new mind-set. Crew co-operation would become the buzz-word; we would have to be polite to navigators; we would need to learn to sympathise with those of them who were failed pilots (the majority); and we would have to shake off much of the hard-earned spirit of independence required in the Lightning world.

Then there were what might be termed local matters. The squadron had been at Gütersloh for a number of years now, we were nicely settled, thank you. Our operations room, positioned upstairs in one of the squadron hangar offices, was an efficient set-up, fine-tuned over the years and working well as an operational hub. The engineering set-up was also good with admirable rapport between our operations and engineering people. Not every squadron could claim that. Neither could every squadron boast the close working relationship we had developed with our ground radar controllers. The ground radar unit, call-sign Backwash, was some distance south of Gütersloh, nonetheless from time to time we had arranged visits and even social events. We found that the Backwash controllers, Luftwaffe officers, had good senses of humour on the whole and were easy to rub along with. One time, during a conversation between a group of our squadron officers and the controllers, the subject of World War Two arose. "Why do your movies always depict us Germans as fools," asked one of the controllers, "surely there is no honour in winning against fools?" There was no answer to this, at least none that we seemed able to drum up on the spot.

The duty ops officer's polite cough interrupted my reflections. I needed to pay heed. "Is there anything else you think you should tell me?" he said.

"The flight went more or less according to plan," I said evasively.

"Glad to hear it," he said. "In that case why…" At this point he was interrupted by the ring of ops telephone. Saved by the bell, I thought. Now I would have a few moments in which to gather my thoughts.

Earlier, the operations officer had briefed me to carry out a practice night interception of a pre-planned high-level, high-speed target. The target would be another Lightning, the interception would take place in a specially designated supersonic area. This area, over a less-densely populated region some 200 miles north of Gütersloh, had clear boundaries which we were not allowed to violate. The first Lightning would take off alone while the other, manned by me, would remain at ground alert until scrambled by Backwash. That was the plan – straightforward, more or less routine, no problem.

When I had walked out to my allocated aircraft via the engineering line hut, I had lingered as I chatted with the engineering line chief. There was no particular rush at that stage in the proceedings. Then, having checked around my Lightning, I had strapped into the cockpit and waited for further orders. Meanwhile, the other Lightning pilot was flying north towards Hamburg to position himself within the supersonic area. While I waited, I double-checked around my cockpit, spoke occasionally with the Backwash controller, and stared at the goings on around me in the brightly-lit aircraft dispersal area. It seemed strange that the equipment, the people and the aircraft I observed were about to be scattered to the four winds. What a waste of effort, I reckoned, and all in the name of so-called progress. And what about me? What about my own future?

My thoughts, suddenly, were disrupted by the Backwash controller. "Standby," he said. "I'll be scrambling you shortly." I signalled to the ground crewman. He stood up and moved closer to the Lightning. In less than a minute, when Backwash had ordered me airborne, I gave a circling motion with one finger to indicate 'engine start' to the ground crewman. He acknowledged and soon, with both engines 'burning and turning', air traffic control had given me clearance to taxi out. My request for an immediate take-off was granted; I could roll straight onto the runway; there were no delays. As I engaged reheats during the take-off run, I made a note that both engine reheats lit and stabilised without difficulty. I would need reliable reheats for this flight.

While I climbed up on a northerly heading, the air traffic controller at Gütersloh instructed me to call Backwash on a tactical frequency. Below, over the high ground to the south and east, a vast undulating sea of cloud was picked out by a combination of moon and stars. Elsewhere, the West German countryside seemed generally cloud-free on a crisp and clear winter's night. The Backwash controller confirmed that he had radar contact with my target which appeared to be, he said, high level and high speed. He ordered me to climb up to 36,000 feet then accelerate to Mach 1.3 in the specified supersonic area. This speed was the most efficient one for supersonic turns in the Lightning. I was instructed to turn twenty degrees as the controller set up the intercept geometry, then thirty degrees. He aimed for a 180 degree interception, which meant that, at precisely the right moment, I had to turn through 180 degrees onto the target's heading. The timing of this turn was crucial: if I turned too soon I could roll out in front of the target (and thereby become a potential target myself), too late and I could end up miles behind the target.

At a range of twenty-five miles I saw the target's 'blip' on my airborne radar. I called "Judy"...no further assistance required from the Backwash controller. The success or failure of the interception was now in my own hands. I held my heading and height for a few more moments as the target's blip, like some creature from outer space, persisted to march down the radar tube. The movement was swift: the target, clearly, was at high speed. It was also, without doubt, at high altitude: the elevation of my radar's scanner confirmed that. Anxiously, I continued to monitor the blip's progress as last-second assessments darted around my mind. There was usually a feeling-in-the-water input despite all of our extensive, expensive training. A difficult intercept could cause headache-inducing mental gyrations – the best antidote for which was probably down to one main factor: long experience as a Lightning pilot. The geometry, unfortunately, for my current case was somewhat flawed because the genius who had worked it out had assumed a high target or a fast target but not really both together.

At what I hoped was impeccable timing, I turned the Lightning. Simultaneously, I eased the twin throttles forward to move them from the mid-range reheat position to maximum power. The Lightning would now act like a pocket rocket although, on the downside, the machine would consume even greater quantities of fuel with even greater rapidity. In the turn,

I applied sixty to seventy degrees angle of bank and before long, as I rolled out, I was gratified to note a distance of a mile or so behind the target: this was pretty much ideal. However, I was now lower and slower than my target which began to pull ahead. With my throttles still at maximum power, I therefore allowed my aircraft to accelerate and climb as I strived to catch up. If this had been for real, if the target had been, say, a Soviet Tupolev Tu-22 'Blinder' with a maximum speed of just over Mach 1.4, my task would have been less problematic. This Lightning target, though, was rather faster and higher and I knew that I faced a struggle to catch up. In the case of the Tupolev, the Soviet machine's maximum height of just over 40,000 feet would, again, have presented me with little difficulty but already I was approaching 10,000 feet higher than that and still needed more.

As I continued to climb and accelerate, I imagined that if this had been for real, if the Soviet machine really *had* been sent on a mission to bomb the hell out of the West, then the Ruhr area might well have been its objective. Indeed, the Tupolev's three-man crew of pilot, navigator and weapons officer would now, presumably, be counting down to bomb or missile release. The Tupolev's twin Dobrynin engines would be at full power. The navigator and weapons officer, sitting within the fuselage in their downwards-firing ejector seats, would set up for the run, make live the relevant switches, tune and retune necessary equipment. Perhaps their eyes would be glued to a meter that indicated range to weapons release. Maybe the pilot, meanwhile, would watch an instrument with a left-right needle to tell him if he needed to adjust his heading. I supposed, in this hypothesis, that the pilot would seek to fly straight and level if possible as he approached weapons release point. In a bomber, stability usually meant accuracy. I speculated on the bomb doors. Presumably, these would have to be opened which might ruffle the bomber's smooth progress through the night air. With the bomb doors locked open, the ugly innards of the Tupolev would be revealed like a dog that bared its teeth before attack. The attack in this case might well come in the form of a nuclear weapon. In the cockpit, the pilot would observe an indicator, perhaps a doll's-eye that flicked from white to black. As the Tupolev drew nearer to weapons release, like the bomber crews of World War Two, the three men on board would try to hold their nerve, not deviate from the desired track as they pressed home their attack. This, at least, should facilitate my job as fighter interceptor.

"You're approaching the southern limit of the supersonic area." This call from the Backwash controller cut through my concentrated (if conjectured) thought processes. A glance at my TACAN navigational aid confirmed the controller's warning. Meantime, the other Lightning pilot cancelled his reheats as he acted on the controller's call. I swiftly caught him up, therefore, 'fired' a missile and called that I had done so. I was now at 56,000 feet and at a speed close to Mach 1.7. I, too, needed to slow down as I came ever-closer to the southern boundary of the supersonic area. There was even the danger that if I overstepped the mark, and went beyond the stipulated boundary, folk at Gütersloh might pick up the sonic double-bang from my aircraft's associated shock waves. I sniggered to myself: talk about going out with a bang – good in some respects, maybe, but I wouldn't have won many friends. Indeed, it might well have put the kibosh on a thing or two. I glanced again at my Machmeter. Even though I had cancelled my reheats by now, a rather too healthy-looking Mach number lingered tiresomely on the gauge. I was already at the maximum-approved height within the supersonic area but that, I felt, was just too bad. My only realistic way to lose all this speed was to climb.

Without further ado, I raised the Lightning's nose to some fifteen degrees angle of climb. Up she went, no bother at all. At around 65,000 feet I squinted at the Machmeter again. The Lightning was still at supersonic speed. So maestro, I thought, you'd better come up with a radical idea – and pretty damn fast. The plan that came to me did so quite quickly even if, with the benefit of hindsight, some might say it was the night's big mistake. I reckoned that if I rolled inverted and pulled the nose down to the horizon, I should be just about subsonic by the time the Lightning started to descend. I calculated that, despite the high altitude, I should retain adequate control during the manoeuvre. I should then, on completion of this course of action, be able to head back towards base in order to land with reasonable levels of fuel reserves. So much for the theory.

The Lightning's height peaked, I estimated, at some 70,000 feet. The view up there, I have to say, was exceptional. To my left (remember I was upside down) I could see the lights of the industrial Ruhr stretch towards the Rhine valley with the Ardennes region of north-east France beyond. To my right side there were fewer lights; the Sauerland plateau and the Weser river valley were identifiable although stretches of cloud still blanketed the area to the south. At this stage I noticed a few more lights, but these were inside my cockpit on the auxiliary warning panel. Seconds later, with these warning lights still on, my main cockpit lighting failed. Immediately, I focussed my attention inside the cockpit where sufficient background lighting allowed me to deduce that both of my engines had flamed out. I was now, in effect, sat inside a flying brick.

On the plus side, the engines were windmilling at high revolutions which ensured that cockpit pressurisation (essential at these high altitudes) was maintained. Equally essential, the pumps for the hydraulically-powered flight controls continued to function – provided the engines continued to windmill at sufficiently high revolutions. My situation was bad but not disastrous. After a second or two of quiet reflection (panic to the layman), I turned off the fuel supply to the engines. The aircraft, not unnaturally, had now entered a rapid rate of descent. At least, I thought, I had plenty of height to lose which meant that, even for a flying brick, there was a little more time for further 'quiet reflection'.

I don't remember exactly when I pressed the engine relight buttons, although I seem to recall seeing Mach 1.3 and 43,000 feet on the flight instruments. When I did press the buttons, the engines fired-up immediately and stayed lit even though I was well outside the flight manual's recommended relight zone. This indeed, I thought, was testimony to the quality of Rolls-Royce engines. I carefully checked each engine in turn but found no signs of ill-effect. After my earlier terse call to the Backwash controller: "Standby – minor problem – call you back," I spoke to him again. This time I assured him that the problem had been solved and that now I was ready to return to base.

Ten minutes later I landed, and ten minutes after that I was in the operations officer's presence. I had resolved to keep mum about what had happened, but clearly he harboured suspicions; something was not quite right. The operations telephone had interrupted his flow of questions but now, with the call over, he appeared determined to persist.

"If the flight went more or less according to plan," he said, "then why the hell have you logged the aircraft altimeter as unserviceable?"

"Because the damn thing was inaccurate."

"How inaccurate?"

"25,000 feet inaccurate."

A pause ensued before the ops officer said: "Now there's a funny thing."

"What do you mean?"

"Well, that's a most unusual fault." He hesitated. "However, I happen to know that it will occur if both engines flame-out above 50,000 feet."

"Oh," I said, "now there's a funny thing."

"Yes," he said. He looked at me, shook his head and continued: "Perhaps we should retire to the mess now?"

"Good plan," I said.

'And by the way,' he said.

"Yes?"

"The beers are on you."

"Okay," I said. I glanced at him and grinned. But I made no further comment.

Chapter 16

A VISIDENT
TOO FAR

Jerry Parr with his wife.

*JERRY PARR SAVED
BY A VICTOR TANKER*

The procedures for a so-called visident, or visual identification by a fighter pilot of an aircraft in flight, should be straightforward. The fighter pilot will position his aircraft adjacent to the other, identify the type, note insignia, tail letters, signs of armament and other details before, if required, he will move to a position where he can be seen by the other pilot. The fighter pilot can then use internationally-agreed signals to give instructions. Used by our fighters when, for example, Soviet Bear and Badger aircraft in the Cold War era flew near to the UK air defence region, the procedures, in theory, should be simple enough. In practice, however, the imponderables are numerous and a fighter pilot's lot is rarely an easy one.

It was one winter's night in the mid-1970s that I was tasked, along with another 23(F) Squadron Lightning pilot, to practise some visidents with a Shackleton aircraft of 8 Squadron. The Shackleton would position itself somewhere over the North Sea, generally to the south of 23 Squadron's base at Leuchars, and the two Lightnings would conduct a variety of interception and visident procedures on the lumbering, four-engine machine. Unkindly dubbed '20,000 rivets flying in approximately close formation', the Avro Shackleton, an aircraft based on the Avro Lincoln (itself derived from the Lancaster heavy bomber of World War Two), was an archaic-looking machine whose intended retirement had been postponed by the need for an AEW (airborne early warning) aircraft to cover the North Sea and northern Atlantic areas. With a cruise speed of around 160 knots, the Shackleton could stay airborne for twelve hours or more (much to the anguish of the ten-man crew who would complain about their cramped and noisy on-board conditions). In addition the machine's slow airspeed meant that Lightning pilots had to be especially perspicacious at night.

I had already flown twice that evening, the time was well past midnight and the engineers were struggling to produce a couple of serviceable Lightnings for the sortie. My enthusiasm for the mission had, frankly, started to wane. Nevertheless, when the engineers finally buzzed through to the squadron operations set-up – "Two aircraft, Mike and Lima, ready" – I had no option but to stir my stumps. I glanced at my fellow pilot whose expression seem to mirror my thoughts: 'Bugger – night flying supper and beer another hour and a bit away.' We picked up our bone domes, checked we had signed the flight authorisation sheet and set off for the engineering line hut. As we signed the relevant logs, we noted that the line chief and his men did not themselves radiate great eagerness for this late-hour flight.

On start-up, my aircraft was fine but the other Lightning had a problem. "I've got a hydraulic leak," said George, the other pilot, "my aircraft is unserviceable." I radioed through to operations:

"George is unserviceable, what do you want me to do?"

"Get airborne anyway," came the reply. Bugger, I thought again, night flying supper...

The pitch-black of the sky seemed particularly uninviting that night as I roared off from Leuchars. I turned onto a southerly heading and was cleared in due course by air traffic control to contact the ground radar controller at Boulmer. The Boulmer controller sounded weary as I checked-in on the radio. "Good evening Mission 23," he said, though his tone suggested: "What the bloody hell are you doing at such an hour?" This was a fair question, I reckoned, though I tried to bolster my spirits and general enthusiasm by considering the mettle of the likes of Douglas Bader, one of my squadron's illustrious forebears, and *'Always on the attack'* – the squadron motto.

"What's my range from the Shackleton now?" I asked the controller.

"He's still south of you, range sixty."

"I'll commence a slow descent in ten miles then."

"Understood. Turn left twenty degrees and you should pick him up on the nose before long."

With the disparity in airspeeds, I would close rapidly from astern. I would have to judge the moment before I started to slow down – not too soon but, perhaps more importantly, not so late that I ended up in an embarrassing rush past the target with no opportunity for a controlled, proficient visident. I was conscious of previous problems on other squadrons, not least the tragic loss of a US exchange officer on 5 Squadron during a night exercise with a Shackleton.

Before long, as predicted by the Boulmer controller, a plump, green blip began to be painted on my radar screen. "Contact with the target," I said to the controller.

"You're still closing quite fast," he said.

I imagined the Shackleton crew in discussion as they monitored my position on their airborne early warning equipment. Surrounded by dials, meters, and knobs, the AEW radar operators, focussed on the screen of their US-designed radar equipment recently recycled from naval Fairey Gannet aircraft, would be watching my every move as they reported back to the rest of the crew. The size of the crew struck me as somewhat lavish. The wartime Lancasters managed with seven men – and that included a couple of gunners. With nearly a dozen men on board one Shackleton, the number seemed a little extravagant, but perhaps I was being naive.

"I'm reducing my airspeed now," I said to the controller. I knew that the controller, like me, would be monitoring the blip movements like a hawk. While my airspeed reduced, I selected flap down as if preparing the Lightning for an approach and landing, although I did not lower my undercarriage. My scan became, in effect, a three-way split between the radar picture, the flight instruments and the occasional glance ahead to try to spot the Shackleton visually. When I did see him, and as the shadowy form transmuted into the Shackleton's bulky shape with distinctive tailplane, straight wings and four engines, I continued to advance with stealth. Before displacing the target to one side of my aircraft, I glanced at the stars and moon to assess the best background light. Then, as I manoeuvred to use this light to advantage, I eased the throttles back to achieve a minimum safe airspeed. That highly critical stage of the visident became a balancing act between operational procedures, safe flying and the achievement of the task.

The Shackleton's heading remained due south as I concluded the first visident which was followed by another one and another one after that, although I forget the total number. I strived to keep a mental plot of my position but my TACAN (tactical air navigational aid) was useless at those low altitudes over the sea and, engrossed as I was in the visident process and perhaps influenced, foolishly, by a touch of professional pride, I failed to ask the Shackleton's navigator for accurate updates of position. At such low altitudes I had no radio contact with the ground controller but when, eventually, I bade goodnight to the Shackleton crew, I climbed up to an altitude where radio reception with Boulmer was resumed and I asked for "pigeons to base".

"Steer 330 degrees," said the Boulmer controller, "your range from Leuchars is 260 miles."

I sensed a chill of apprehension. Despite the Shackleton's slow airspeed, we had wandered further south than I had reckoned and a quick mental calculation followed by another now confirmed the awful truth: I had insufficient fuel to make it home. In a shamefaced tone I revealed my problem to the Boulmer controller. "Standby," he said, followed by: "Leeming's available as a diversion airfield but wait one…sorry, Mission 23…Leeming is about the same distance from you as Leuchars."

To help conserve fuel I shut down one engine while I took stock of my situation. Positioned miles out over the sea and about forty miles short of any suitable airfield I was, without doubt, in trouble. Almost the worst aspect was that it was entirely my own fault. With my options looking bleaker by the minute, I began mentally to rehearse my emergency drills. I would aim to fly towards the coast, descend to around 10,000 feet, then turn through 180 degrees to point the Lightning out to sea while I ejected close to the shoreline. I spoke again with the Boulmer controller who confirmed that relevant authorities had been made aware of my situation, overdue procedures were in hand, and the search and rescue helicopter had been alerted. In my mind, I went through my prospective ejection drills and dinghy drills when, suddenly, a new voice on the aircraft radio interrupted my dismal thought processes: "Boulmer radar, good evening, this is Victor 45. I gather you have a Lightning with a fuel emergency?"

"Affirmative, Victor 45," said the controller, "the Lightning's callsign is Mission 23."

"Mission 23 this is Victor 45, I can offer you an in-flight refuel if you wish?"

"Thanks Victor 45," I said, "I'd better take up your offer ASAP please." At once, the Boulmer controller gave me a heading to steer towards the Victor and, as I set off, I heaved a great sigh of relief. I began to thank my lucky stars; I thanked them as I'd never thanked them before. In truth, I could barely believe my luck. I was here, in the middle of the North Sea in the middle of winter, in the middle of the night, when, like some high-octane fairy godmother, a Victor tanker had happened to appear, suddenly and seemingly out of nowhere, to save my bacon. I experienced a strangely ephemeral sensation as if some pivotal presence, some clandestine omniscience, had conspired to see me through.

My difficulties, however, were not over yet. The next problem, to ensure a successful in-flight refuel, would require me to hold my nerve. Any rough flying on my part or any actions which might cause me to fail to make contact with the flight-refuelling basket would only make the situation worse. The pressure, as they say, was on. As the controller counted down my range from the Victor, and as the Victor's radar return appeared on my radar screen, I checked and double-checked the necessary cockpit settings before the flight refuelling. The Victor crew had done their stuff too: the flight-refuelling hoses were deployed already, the Victor was on a steady heading, so the captain cleared me for an immediate refuel. I kept telling myself to relax as I eased the Lightning's refuelling probe towards the basket. Night refuelling is much harder than in daylight but I forced myself to concentrate on the correct techniques: don't stare at the basket; focus on the Victor's lights; don't be put off by any bright stars in the background. Suddenly I felt a satisfying 'clunk', a sign that the probe and basket had made good contact, and I knew that my main task now was to fly smoothly, to hold the correct position in order to facilitate fuel transfer from Victor to Lightning. When a glance at my fuel gauges indicated that this was happening and that the fuel gauges had started to move in the desired direction at last, I felt able to heave a second sigh of relief.

Later, when I was back at base and, finally, I could tuck into that night flying supper and mug of beer, I mulled the incident over and over in my mind. I still felt shocked by my own foolishness. I knew I wanted to escape that feeling but I knew, too, that it would be impossible. It was not un-usual, so I was told, to look over the shoulder after such an experience. I had acquired lessons at different levels. I had learnt about incomplete as-sumptions, about the hollow sensation when options begin to look limited, about the reserves of courage, and infinity of effort needed when those op-tions start to dry up. I had learnt, too, about the personal inner depths discovered by those taken to the brink. I began to realise that desperate, dismal, forlorn situations would compel an individual to probe those inner depths but I knew too, that the result was more or less bound to be ben-eficial in the end.

Chapter 17

TIMELY
TELEPATHY

Stephen Gyles in an 11 Squadron Lightning.

STEVE GYLES IN A JAM

The Germans appear to appreciate straight lines. While the British, on the other hand, cannot resist building curves into their roads, the Germans, like the Romans before them, preferred to take the traveller from A to B in as direct a way as possible. The German canal system is no exception to this general rule and when I reflect on that fateful day in mid-February 1974, a day of such curious coincidences, and when I think of my wife Anita's quarter-mile dash along the canal bank when every second seemed to count, I feel sure she was assisted by this straight Teutonic trait. What compelled her to make that dash with our eighteen-month-old child Paul clutched in her arms, however, is a mystery and, I suppose, will always remain so.

121

That day had started well enough. It was a Friday morning, the February air was crisply cold but the airfield staff at Gütersloh appeared geared-up to cope with the challenges of a Nordrhein-Westfalen winter. At that stage in my career I was a reasonably experienced Lightning operator with a tour on 11(F) Squadron at Leuchars in Scotland under my belt, followed by a two-year spell as a Lightning simulator instructor at Gütersloh.

My ambition to become a fighter pilot went back a number of years. At school I had always liked aircraft and told everyone that I was going to be a pilot, although the start of my air force career, in truth, had been prompted by a fellow student at Enfield Grammar School. This young fellow announced one day as we sat in the school library that he had applied to join the air force as an engineering officer. At that point I was still contemplating my future, so I felt intensely irritated by this lad's sudden announcement. If I was to apply to join the RAF, how dare he beat me to it? Without further ado, I sent in my application that very day. As it turned out, this fellow and I ended up on the same selection course at RAF Biggin Hill. He lasted one day although I managed the full five-day process at the end of which I was one of six to be accepted (sixty had applied in total).

By 1974, some nine years on from those days, I was very happy with life at Gütersloh. There was a close-knit community there, I had been married for about three years and my wife Anita seemed to enjoy the married quarters camaraderie. She had become used to the noise of aircraft activity and she took scant interest in daily flying routines. She was unaware, therefore, that I had been programmed to lead a four-ship section of Lightnings on that particular Friday morning. My task was to fly with the other three aircraft up to the designated North Sea firing range, north-west of Gütersloh. When cleared by the range officer we would descend to low level, down to a height of about 250 feet, where we would fire our Aden cannon into the sea. The experience could be exhilarating and we looked forward to a change from our usual high-level work.

In the end our plans, fortunately, were thwarted by bad weather. I say fortunately because without doubt the events that followed would have proved fatal at low level. Cloudy conditions forced us to a height of around 20,000 feet to carry out our firings, but even at that altitude the sortie's objective could still be achieved. When cleared to proceed by the range officer, I ordered the four-ship formation into an echelon starboard formation position. The members of the formation acknowledged and a quick glance over my shoulder confirmed when the aircraft were in position. I rechecked my cockpit switches, double-checked that the firing area was cloud free and prepared to break hard to port. The time was just before 0930.

Meanwhile, Anita was in the RAF Gütersloh post office. Paul was proving to be a handful, typical of a toddler, but she had become adept at coping with him. In any case, there were plenty of other young children around and mums would readily close ranks, unfazed by rowdy kids. An attitude of mutual encouragement and practical co-operation helped to promote a good social life on the station so that even a trip to the post office could turn out to be quite a sociable occasion. Anita had parked our car just outside the building. She knew that I was proud of this car and although hardly the car-keen type herself, she was aware that cars were a particular issue for service personnel in Germany. As long as laid-down regulations were followed, servicemen and servicewomen posted to Germany could buy tax free cars. Most of us, therefore, enjoyed cars of a better standard than we could afford in the UK. Furthermore, every month we could apply for an entitled allocation of fuel vouchers for use at certain petrol stations. With tax free cars, discounted fuel and various other perks, the material side of life had distinct advantages for those of us posted to Germany.

One downside was the housing situation back at home where rampant inflation meant that those who did not own a property found it ever harder, as time went by, to get started on the dreaded property ladder. Some, though, seemed to block this reality from their minds and took the view that it was better to make the most of the here-and-now. With everyone posted to Germany required, more or less, to live in married quarters, at least a strong and thriving sense of community was encouraged. This was backed by the BFG (British Forces Germany) set-up with its own radio station, schools, postal system and other facilities designed to look after service families. In addition, there were further great opportunities such as visits to West Berlin by the comfortable and free military train, and in the winter months good skiing could be enjoyed at Winterberg and Willingen to the south of Gütersloh. In short, life in Germany was good and perhaps this was on Anita's mind when she stood in the post office.

Something else, though, was about to strike Anita's mind, something that would enter her thought processes with such ferocity and in such a way as to make her heart leap up to her mouth. Perhaps, when it happened, a hum of conversation buzzed in the background, or perhaps a melody might have rung out, something joyful to capture the eternal spirit. Maybe, at that precise moment in time, a mundane yet specific incident might have caught her attention, like a motorbike roar or someone wearing a brightly coloured scarf. Maybe everything just went eerily quiet. Perhaps, out of the blue, came snatches of old memories in curiously distorted and whimsical form. The phenomenon, when it happened, was at once deeply moving and thoroughly disturbing; in her own words she felt, 'a sudden and compelling urge' to see me land. She grabbed Paul and clutched him tenaciously, linking her fingers together around his small waist as if to prevent an alarming accident. "Come on, Paul," she whispered, "we must go to the car."

Later, when Anita and I compared notes, we worked out that this was the moment at which I had transmitted a Mayday call on the radio. The seconds immediately before had seemed unexceptional. I knew that modifications to the Aden cannon had been carried out in efforts to deal with 'rising arch' stoppages, and I knew that when I broke away from the formation and pulled the firing trigger I had to monitor my 'g' meter carefully. The engineers had briefed us to apply about 3 g as we fired the cannon. This would prove the success or otherwise of the cannons' modification. I heard the noise as my cannons fired initially, then the noise ceased abruptly. Simultaneously the aircraft nose dropped, the Lightning went into a steep spiral dive and entered cloud. I tried to correct the dive but found that the ailerons were jammed hard left, as was the rudder. At once, I put out a Mayday call and advised the controller of imminent ejection. In a last-gasp attempt, I put both hands on the control column to try to coerce some movement of the ailerons. Suddenly, I found that by using all of my strength I could force, by a series of jerks, the ailerons towards a central position.

Gradually, I managed to bring the aircraft under control and to pull out of the dive. Still in cloud, I climbed from around 12,000 feet back up to my original cloud-free altitude of 20,000 feet. I made a further radio call to arrange for another Lightning from the formation to inspect my aircraft for signs of damage. With my jerky aileron movements and rudder still jammed fully to the left, the other Lightning flew, understandably, towards my machine in a rather tentative manner. The other pilot, though, reported no signs of obvious external damage. We therefore decided that the other three aircraft should return to base ahead of me while I tested my Lightning to work out the best method of approach and landing.

By this stage Anita had strapped Paul into his seat before she returned hastily to her own car seat. She roared off in a great hurry, away from the post office building to join the public highway just outside the station entrance gates. She drove at speed for about a mile, then veered off the road onto the verge where she decided to abandon the car. Having grabbed Paul from his seat she stumbled up a canal bank where she reckoned to be able to see the airfield. At the top of the bank she found that she could, indeed, obtain a reasonable overall view although the key spot, the runway threshold, seemed distant. However, she noted that since the line of the canal ran, straight as a dye, along the airfield boundary, she could improve her vantage point by running along the canal bank for a distance of about a quarter of a mile. This would take her close to the runway threshold. With Paul in her arms it would be a struggle but she knew, somehow, that the situation was urgent and that time was of the essence; she was still driven by her experience in the post office – that desperate urge to see me land. At this point in time, of course, she had no knowledge of where I was or what I was up to, or even if I was airborne. Her 'compelling urge' was pure telepathic instinct.

In my Lightning, I continued to assess different combinations of speed and flight control input. There was nothing in any manual to guide me; the circumstances were unique and it was up to me to work out the best course of action, although I had discussions with base about possible methods of approach and landing. We decided, eventually, to have the approach-end crash barrier removed and the approach-end cable rigged. With this done and with my aircraft's hook lowered, I would aim for a cable engagement to bring the Lightning to as rapid a stop as possible. There was a chance, however, that the aircraft's fast approach speed might lead to hook structural failure. My intention, therefore, was to land in the asphalt undershoot area just before the runway threshold in order to give me a run of about 1,300 feet before cable engagement. This distance, I hoped, should slow the Lightning enough to reduce the chance of hook structural failure.

Meantime, as Anita persevered with her dash along the canal bank, she tried to calm Paul. The more she attempted to hasten, the heavier the child seemed to become. She wondered about the airfield security set-up. If someone spotted her running along the airfield boundary fence with what must have looked like a large package, it would, surely, have appeared highly suspicious. The IRA were up to all sorts of tricks these days; only the previous month a gang had hijacked a helicopter in County Donegal and used it to bomb the police. Maybe just now a local controller in the air traffic control tower was observing her through binoculars. Perhaps a police vehicle would race up soon and ask her to explain herself. And what would she say? She had been in the post office when a mysterious force suddenly wanted her to see her husband land his Lightning? "Okay, madam," the RAF policeman might ask, "so when did your husband get airborne and what time do you expect him to return for the landing?" As she ran, one moment thoughts flooded her mind and a maelstrom of memories was awakened, the next moment her mind went blank. It was as if she was caught up in some fantastic dream. Nothing, however, appeared to dampen or modify the urge to reach the demanded spot ahead. An unremarkable, treeless patch of grassy ground had become an irresistible objective and she must have felt as though she was being driven forward by some ethereal, hidden hand.

From my cockpit perspective, by now I had managed to descend through the cloud without significant problems and I had worked out a realistic combination of speed and control input. I felt fairly confident about my progress so I decided to aim, as far as possible, to follow SOPs (standard operating procedures) even though my situation was far from standard. I made radio calls at standard reporting points and I noted that the controller, when he replied, sounded deliberately unflustered although I was aware of unusual background chatter. The air traffic controllers, I assumed, had been joined by experts who would try to offer specialist advice. By about twelve miles from touchdown I was lined up with the runway and able to maintain reasonable directional control. I knew, however, that continued control of my aircraft was highly tenuous and that I might be forced to eject at any moment, even so I never lost hope that I would be able to pull off a successful landing.

Anita was breathless as she ran along the canal bank, nevertheless she felt buoyed up as her aiming point loomed. The timing was crucial, she did not know why, but she did know that every second counted if she was to be there on time. A chilly February wind soughed through the grass as she dashed along, and she hugged Paul close to her, anxious to protect him from the bitter breezes. She had to watch her step on the slippery track. At one stage, when distracted by the noise of aircraft, she glanced up to observe three Lightnings turn sharply overhead. The aircraft then lined themselves up with the runway before they landed in close succession. She did not, though, stop running; she still had a distance of about 100 yards to go.

I was some miles from the runway touchdown point when I lowered the undercarriage and the flaps. I was prepared for problems and I would have raised the flaps if required but this proved unnecessary as I continued to retain control of the aircraft. When the runway came in sight I eased the Lightning down gradually, lower than normal as I aimed for touchdown in the undershoot area. The miles ticked by one by one, and while I persisted with the long, straight-in approach, I felt rising tension as the *moment critique* drew near. Although I had to struggle with the controls, my concentration was so intense that I was not conscious of an overly firm grip on the stick, like that of a rookie pilot. I was not even aware of a solitary figure near the runway threshold, a young mother who stood with a child clutched in her arms as she strained to observe my landing.

Instinctively, Anita let out a small cry of horror when she saw a 'drunken, wallowing Lightning' come in low above her head. She had just reached the vantage point and as she continued to hold Paul tightly, her immediate inclination was to duck in order to protect him. She felt the potential of a terrible darkness, the grey fog of an aching, empty heart; an incongruous, poignant air of trepidation. When the Lightning touched down she saw sparks fly up from a hook attached to the machine's rear, and she saw the hook bounce back into the air. As the hook failed to catch a cable strung across the runway, the Lightning then careered down the runway with several fire engines in hot pursuit. When she saw the Lightning come to a halt at the far end of the runway she could, at last, sigh with relief as she felt an inexplicable, overwhelming surge of gratitude rise within her...*now all will be well...all will be well...all will be well.*

I touched down in the asphalt undershoot area as planned but my ongoing struggle with the controls resulted in a firmer landing than usual. Just after touchdown, I stop-cocked both engines and tried to keep the Lightning straight as the aircraft rushed towards the cable. Anticipating a sudden deceleration as the hook caught the cable, I braced myself. When nothing happened, I realised that the hook must have skipped over the cable so, at once, I deployed the tail parachute. With my rudder still jammed fully to the left, I could use the left brake only. However, with a crosswind from the right, the tail chute, luckily, caused the aircraft to weathercock to the right. This meant that I could use the left brake in a series of dabs to help slow the Lightning. I managed, consequently, to hold a fairly straight line down the runway before the aircraft entered the upwind barrier at a speed of about thirty knots. Eventually, when I was surrounded by fire engines and when crews ran up to help release me from the cockpit, it dawned on me that my firm grip on the control stick could finally be released.

Later, when the engineers explained what had gone wrong, I realised again how close I had come to the edge. The squadron senior engineering officer told me that pip pins, designed to secure a chute that was part of the spent cartridge collector system, had not been pushed home fully. Gun vibration had caused the pins to fall out, the chute had then dislodged and impinged on a fibreglass shroud that covered the three flight control rods in that area. A build-up of spent cartridges and links had forced the chute ever-harder against the shroud until its distorted shape began to act like a calliper brake on the rudder and aileron control rods, although the elevator rod, mercifully, had been unaffected. Some weeks later the squadron commander told me that I had been awarded a 'green endorsement' for my actions during the episode. At the time, however, the squadron commander, perhaps conscious of how close he had come to having to break alternative news to Anita, suggested that I went home to see her.

When I let myself into our married quarter, I was aware at once of the contrast between the frenetic scenes at work and the cosy, familiar atmosphere here at home. I could hear Paul's gurgles and splutters as he coped with his lunch. I must have wondered, I suppose, about the best way to explain what had happened for I recall that I hesitated for a second or two. When I joined my wife and son, Paul immediately beamed and pointed. Anita looked at me and smiled. She stood up and we hugged. I don't think I said very much initially, but perhaps there was something about her expression that told me she knew already. It was not until after lunch, when Paul was asleep and Anita and I could talk without interruption, that we could analyse with amazement our uncanny, impromptu exercise of telepathic co-ordination.

Later that evening, when Anita took Paul up to bed, I remained downstairs for a few moments of reflection. I remember how, as I stared through a window at the February scene outside, the leafless trees and icy surrounds seemed surreal. A ghost-like wind whistled through the roof rafters. I spotted an old green moped chug past our married quarter, its rider bent forward intently. I thought how small and frail the driver looked, so light and vulnerable against the elements yet he appeared to drive on with a confidence that never for a single moment failed him.

Chapter 18

FINE ART

*Chris Stone, Officer Commanding
23 Squadron, 1970.*

*CHRIS STONE
RECALLS
A CLOSE SHAVE*

Perhaps I was being unreasonable. After all, a great deal of anger still raged within me and maybe I should have waited until we were inside the briefing room's calmer atmosphere before the bombshell was delivered. However, my impatience seemed well-nigh impossible to contain; I held in my mind a fleeting image, one which recurred over and over, an image which persisted to stoke up my fury even more. Eventually, as he climbed down the ladder attached to the side of his Lightning and as he looked at me quizzically, I broke the news. The young pilot's face turned an ashen colour. He was clearly innocent, I thought, but even so my annoyance was hard to

129

appease. No doubt, I reflected later, a person brought close to a premature and gratuitous death displays a particularly unforgiving form of wrath.

At that point in time I had been a fighter pilot in the Royal Air Force for nearly twenty years and I was in that most valued of appointments for a fighter pilot – the commanding officer of a Lightning squadron. Having been born and raised in East Anglia where, in my formative years, I had witnessed the build-up of World War Two airfields on farmland around my home, my association with aircraft and flying were, in a sense, in the blood. I can still recall the events quite clearly at one particular airfield, barely a three-mile cycle ride from my home, when high excitement was stirred-up as a fighter wing of P-51 Mustangs of the 8th US Air Force arrived in 1943.

One day I decided with a few friends to cycle to the airfield in order to see what was going on there. We had just reached the airfield boundary, almost up to the end of the runway, when a P-51 Mustang aircraft suddenly crashed across the country lane right in front of us. We were a group of ten-year-olds and we could barely believe our eyes. As the Mustang continued to charge over our quiet country lane, a wing was deposited in a ditch while the remaining fuselage hurtled through a hedge before it came to rest in a field. Our group of youngsters gawked, mouths ajar, at this incredible scene. We seemed struck dumb but our amazement, though, was not about to end. When the dust began to settle, we watched as the pilot released his straps from the Mustang's wrecked cockpit, jumped clear and calmly lit up a Lucky Strike cigarette as he walked away. We still said nothing but thoughts of hero-worship undoubtedly beat fast in each of our young hearts. One youngster in particular seemed to make the conscious decision right there and then that, come what may, he would be a pilot one day.

After this, it was perhaps inevitable that our group of impressionable schoolboys should continue to cycle regularly to the airfield to observe events. After a few months the Mustangs moved out to be replaced by a medium bomber group of four squadrons of B-26 Marauders from the 9th US Air Force. We did not know at the time that we were witnesses to the build-up towards D-Day. We saw bombers being refuelled, or bombed-up, or returning from sorties with signs of battle damage after missions to strike at German defences or to hit lines of communication before the invasion itself in June 1944.

Years later, I depicted the scene in an oil painting entitled 'When I Grow Up' (exhibited by the American Society of Aviation Artists in the year 2000). The painting showed a B-26 Marauder on a hardstand while a young lad (me!) sat on his bicycle as, enthralled, he watched the goings-on.

When I Grow Up, painting by Chris Stone.

In 1951 I left high school and, as I vowed all those years before, applied to join the Royal Air Force as a pilot. Fortunately I was accepted and sent to Cottesmore to train on Harvard aircraft. After training, I was posted to a fighter squadron, then further postings to various other fighter squadrons ensued. During this time I flew Meteor aircraft, F-86 Sabres, and Hunters. Eventually I was posted as an instructor with the Day Fighter Combat School at the Central Fighter Establishment. Then, in 1967, sixteen years after I had left school, I was posted to RAF Wattisham in Suffolk where, as a flight commander on 111(F) Squadron, I would fly the Lightning Mark 3. A highlight of my tour at Wattisham was to fly as number three in a four-ship formation on a station open day. Later, I portrayed the four-ship's dramatic stream take-off in an oil painting which now hangs in the RAF Club, Piccadilly, London.

After three years with 111 Squadron, I was posted as commanding officer of 23(F) Squadron equipped with the Lightning Mark 6 and based at RAF Leuchars in Scotland. I was still fairly new in my job when, one day, I briefed a young first-tour pilot for a sortie that would include low-level interceptions followed by intruder identification (a procedure known as 'visident' or visual identification). The weather that day was good – a fine, clear-blue sky at Leuchars with, to the east, scattered cumulus cloud between 2,000 and 5,000 feet. The two fighters would take turns to be target and interceptor and, as we would be operating below ground radar cover, we would have to rely on the Lightning's airborne radar. This could produce problems because the aircraft radar, known as AI 23B, had an unfortunate tendency at low altitude to lock-on to the surface of the sea instead of onto the target itself. The effect of this could be to mislead the interceptor pilot into believing that his target remained at a constant distance and that, if his Lightning was to have any hope of catching the target, he needed to increase airspeed.

The sortie that day went well at first. We carried out three successful intercept runs and were ready to set up for a fourth. It was my turn to act as target. In the pre-flight briefing we had agreed that the target, to create more of a challenge for the interceptor, would not call details of airspeed and altitude on the aircraft radio. For this fourth run I opted for an altitude of 1,000 feet and the relatively low airspeed of 275 knots. I set up these parameters, then sat there flying along fat, dumb and happy as any good target should do. Meanwhile, I used my own AI 23B in 'search' mode to monitor the area ahead in case of any conflicting air traffic. After a while I heard the other pilot call 'splash', a term used in peacetime to indicate that a missile launch could have been made. Good, I thought, all's going fine.

I was continuing to fly along, quietly enjoying the ride, when my peace was suddenly and violently shattered – indeed, like a bolt out of the blue. I experienced three main sensations. I heard a loud roar and a whooshing noise (this, despite the sound protection of my bone-dome). There was a vicious upwards thrust on my Lightning – a feeling similar, I imagined, to the kick up the backside that must be felt at the moment of pulling an ejection seat handle. Then, at the same split-second moment in time, I caught a clear, never-to-be-forgotten, glimpse of the other pilot's bone-dome as it flashed by slightly below and to the left of my aircraft.

It took some seconds for me to regain my composure, but when my heart had stopped pounding I called my number two on the radio. By now he was disappearing rapidly into the wide blue yonder (I learnt later that his airspeed was around the 450 knot mark). "The exercise is over," I said tersely, "climb up to 25,000 feet and we'll rendezvous before RTB (return to base)."

"Copied," he said.

Rash thoughts now rebounded through my head. Surely, I thought, nobody would dare to buzz another aircraft in such a reckless manner, especially an aircraft flown by his boss. Perhaps this young lad thought he should try to push the boundaries, show who was really the boss. My cage had been seriously rattled and this, no doubt, allowed such thoughts, no matter how perverse, to race through my mind. I could see, however, that as the lad still

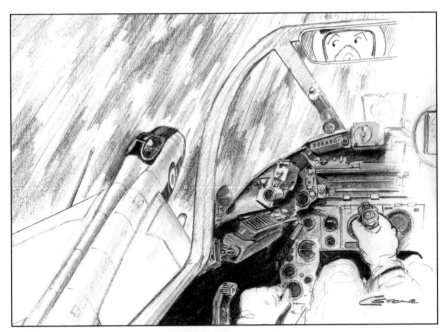

Sketch for Fine Art... I heard a loud roar and a whooshing noise...

hurtled along in the same direction and that, since there was no sign of him pulling up to perform some kind of idiotic victory roll, this at least should provide a measure of cold comfort. On later reflection, when I pondered the level of professionalism instilled on all within the Lightning force, I realised that these early thoughts were fired more by fury than by logic. At the time, though, I couldn't be sure about anything apart from the fact that, but for a few inches to spare, both aircraft and both pilots would have joined the annals of missing aircraft mysteries.

When we were back on the ground, and when I saw from the young pilot's reaction that he had absolutely no idea of the near-disaster he had caused, I think I must have begun to calm down slowly. Later assessment of his radar film confirmed the false lock situation. The squadron weapons instructor lectured us all again about the pitfalls of low-level visidents and he reminded us how to spot the signs when the AI 23B tiresomely locked-on to the sea's surface. As for the young lad involved, he was mortified about what had happened, and I suspected that he might have been even more mortified if he had known my initial reactions.

The Lightning's airborne radar was designed to allow the pilot to intercept and identify another aircraft in any conditions, day or night, rain or shine, cloudy or clear. To practise for the worst conditions, therefore, pilots were encouraged to conduct their interceptions by means of radar alone –

in other words, with their heads buried inside cockpits. For some of the older hands like me, this could go against the grain. We had been taught from square one that a good fighter pilot should keep his head out of the office, should use the good old eyeball Mark 1 to scan the skies constantly for signs of other aircraft. In the Lightning we would work to use our AI 23Bs to best advantage, however we were not averse to the odd visual peep outside the cockpit to confirm what the radar told us. The aphorism that, 'one peep was worth a thousand sweeps', became quite common within the Lightning world.

When I thought about this and when I reflected on the close call we had experienced, I could not escape the conclusion that a sneaky peep on that day would surely have been justified. After all, this simple expedient might potentially have saved the lives of two pilots and avoided the loss of two valuable aircraft. And who would wish to argue with that?

The line between realism in training and realities in the air could, on occasions, be hard to define. Striking the right balance could sometimes prove to be quite a fine art.

Chapter 19

VIVE LA DIFFERENCE

Dave Bramley, while attending a course in preparation for a job in the RAF Careers Information Service.

DAVE BRAMLEY IN A FRAUGHT FRENCH FORMATION

It was in the early 1970s, when I was a pilot on 29(F) Squadron, that my boss handed me the buff-coloured envelope. The message, he said, was an important one. The night-flying programme had just been completed and a few colleagues watched as I tore open the envelope to find a curt note inside: 'You are posted to Colmar-Meyenheim, Alsace, France.' I turned to ask the boss if he knew the whereabouts of this Colmar-Whatsisname. He did not, which surprised me slightly (Lightning bosses were supposed to know everything). Together, therefore, we dug out some maps and located the French air force base some forty miles south of Strasbourg and adjacent to the Rhine valley and where, as a member of the second squadron of the thirteenth wing (otherwise

135

known as *Deux treize*), I would fly Mirage aircraft.

It was a year or so later on a fine spring day in 1971, by which time I had qualified as an operational pilot with *Deux treize*, that I became ensnared in the most bizarre and hazardous situation that had, at the root, the barriers of different languages as one of the causes of near-calamity. The experience that day was a seminal moment for me; one of those times in life when you pause to take stock and learn for the future. A moment which, on reflection, could seem quite surreal.

Later, I would find myself caught off-guard when a discussion with a particular individual, or perhaps a certain set of circumstances, suddenly took me back to those barriers and to that event in 1971. Such occasions might, in turn, trigger memories of the days when I first contemplated joining the RAF; days when I had not in my wildest dreams imagined that I would become a fighter pilot, let alone an exchange officer with the French air force. Unlike quite a few who joined the service, I did not have an air force family background, I was not born with an inner, uncontrollable urge to fly, in truth I could hardly grasp the concept. I did not even have early experience through National Service as the requirement for this duty was abandoned just before the end of my schooldays.

If my reasons for joining the service were unusual, at least this engendered an open-minded approach towards the motives of others. It was later in my air force career, when I became head of the London Area Careers Information Service and when I listened to hundreds of applicants who wished to join the Royal Air Force, that I learnt much about many different people. I learnt, especially, not to be hasty to judge peoples' motives. I listened to reasons for wanting to become a member of Her Majesty's forces which ranged from the inspirational to the incredible. However, despite the diversity of explanation, it was the determination of so many to become air force pilots that made me feel proud to be one myself.

This feeling was reinforced when put in context with my own reasons for joining – not only unorthodox but also, frankly, rather less than inspirational. When I left school I had applied for a place at Loughborough University where, after a three-year course, I gained a degree in physical education before I became a teacher in a London school. I learned then about the Royal Air Force's need for physical education specialists to train as parachute instructors at their parachute school at Abingdon where, as it happened, I was born. The advertisements made this sound like a fabulous way to earn a living and definitely much better than teaching gymnastics skills to tiresome kids. The reality, I discovered later, was somewhat different, indeed my early parachute experiences felt far from fabulous.

A further aspect on my personal agenda was to be able to continue to play top-class hockey. Having captained Loughborough and played for the English Universities and several county teams, I was aware that the RAF team at that time was one of the best in the country. I therefore answered the advertisement, applied to join the Royal Air Force to become a parachute instructor (i.e. to jump out of aircraft not to sit in and steer them) and was accepted – and in time captained the RAF hockey team which won the inter-service championship of that year.

I had not been in the parachute world long before I was invited to apply for the RAF's flying branch. Not enough potential pilots, so it seemed, were making it through the hurdles of the aircrew selection process. To put it another way, the air force was desperate. The all-jet training system was under way by then and eventually I made it to the Lightning operational conversion unit at RAF Coltishall in Norfolk before my posting to the newly-reformed 29(F) Squadron at RAF Wattisham in Suffolk. Towards the end of this tour, in late 1969, I received hints that I was in line for an exchange tour. I assumed this would be an exchange with the United States Air Force as we were buying F4 Phantom aircraft at the time, and in any case I did not realise that we had exchanges with anyone else. I was more than surprised, therefore, when Wing Commander Brian Carroll handed me the fateful piece of paper with news of my posting to Colmar.

As I could not speak a word of French at that point, my first port of call was to the Language Tuition Centre on Oxford Street, London. After two months there, I left for France in May 1970. My wife and (now) three kids would follow in September. My arrival in France, at the Mirage aircraft operational conversion unit near Dijon, was seriously inauspicious. During my pre-arrival briefings, the British Embassy in Paris had been at pains to stress that I should follow certain protocols at French air force bases. In particular, it was most important that I should present myself in working hours to the base commander before I went anywhere or did anything on his base. There had been recent lapses in this procedure and the matter was becoming political.

I travelled by train from Paris to Dijon and when, late-ish on a Friday night, the train pulled-in at Dijon railway station I was met by a senior pilot from the operational conversion unit. This man gabbled away nineteen to the dozen but regretfully, despite all of my intensive training at the language school, I did not understand a word he said. I did, however, gather that this hardly mattered as I was invited immediately to a party in the crewroom where everyone was incoherent anyway. The party was being hosted by a visiting Belgian Mirage 3 Squadron and my first duty was to represent the United Kingdom in an international *escargot* eating contest. In more ways than one, including my failure formally to meet the base commander, the scene had begun to look like a Friday night horror show.

Nonetheless, by around midnight I was beginning to feel rather well integrated despite having come a resounding last in the contest. The Franco-Belgian hospitality seemed to be doing the trick, I thought, when suddenly I noticed in front of me the tall, distinguished figure of the base commander in colonel's uniform. The colonel stood and stared. At once, I stumbled out some idiot French phrases. The colonel still stood and stared. "This is very unexpected," I droned on, practically wringing my hands in woe. I took some minor comfort from the fact that it was late, the party was wild and he was still there. And sure enough, when I presented myself formally on the following Monday morning, he had an amused twinkle in his eye and his welcome was outstanding – a sense of welcome, incidentally, which has been replicated virtually everywhere I have been in France ever since. (After my service career I formed a defence/aerospace consultancy company in Paris, I also bought and sold property and still, in 2011, own a property by the sea in Normandy.)

Hard work soon began. The Mirage 3, like the Lightning, was essentially an air defence fighter. The Mirage 3's delta wing gave the aircraft a remarkably stable weapons' platform for both air-to-air and air-to-ground missile firing, tasks the *Deux treize* carried out in roughly equal parts; they applied, in other words, versatility – *la polyvalence* (try saying that after a few beers). The downside of the aircraft was its fairly unsophisticated weaponry and an engine that was prone to compressor stall at low airspeed.

On completion of the course at Dijon I moved to Colmar where, reunited with my family, we began to relish the French way of life. My wife, as a keen bridge player, joined a local bridge club where she was eager to demonstrate her mastery of the game. While contemplating tactics for her first hand she suddenly realised that she had not the faintest idea about the French words for hearts, diamonds, clubs, spades – not to mention any other necessary phrases such as 'no trumps'. Undaunted, she carried on regardless and, just as I did, learnt by plunging in at the deep end and hoping for the best. After a few months we were both fluent in French and language was no longer an issue.

As a recently operational Lightning pilot, the *Deux Treize* knew I would be a useful 'secret weapon' to them when the announcement came through of a squadron visit by 111(F) Squadron (Treble One Squadron, otherwise known as 'Tremblers'), then equipped with Lightning aircraft. In particular, I would be able to offer advice on tactics for practice combat sorties of Lightning vs. Mirage. Not long after Tremblers' arrival a high altitude four-ship combat sortie was scheduled – two Lightnings pitted against two Mirage 3s. The plan was to take off in a two-pairs trail formation from Colmar's runway 02 (aligned roughly north/south along the Rhine valley), then turn due west as we climbed above the Vosges mountains. Once at a height of around 30,000 feet the Lightnings and Mirage 3s would split away from each other before, after a suitable interval, they turned back to commence 'battle'. That, at least, was the plan.

The high-level part of this plan seemed to go reasonably well at first. In the Mirage 3 camp we had Sergent-Chef Marion as the leader, with me as his number two. The Lightning pair was led by an experienced operator, Tony Alcock. One problem, though, soon emerged: Sergent-Chef Marion insisted on pursuing a rear-attack profile even though our opponents had already called 'Fox 1'. That is, they had released forward-firing missiles and Marion's rear attack was pointless as he and I had already been shot down (theoretically, that is). The good sergent-chef appeared not to understand this, or not to care about it, or both.

Eventually, after more cavorting around French airspace, the time came to recover to Colmar. Our intention was for three aircraft to descend in a vic formation with one Lightning holding a position about half-a-mile astern. We aimed to penetrate a cloud layer before we conducted a flypast at Colmar airfield. However...somehow, somewhere, what should have been a perfectly straightforward procedure managed to turn itself into one of extraordinary complexity. By a series of curious, unplanned manoeuvres as we descended towards Colmar, Marion and I ended up in different formation positions from those at the start. Tony Alcock in his Lightning still led the formation and was therefore in charge of radio and navigational aspects. However, now Marion was on the leader's starboard wing while I, still in my Mirage 3 (although the way events were to pan out, almost anything seemed possible), held an echelon port position on the lead Lightning. The other Lightning, as briefed, maintained a distance some half-a-mile astern the rest of our formation.

Under the control of Colmar radar, with our new-look formation just above the cloud layer, a number of unexpected things, in true 'snafu' style, now happened all at once. First of all the good sergent-chef announced that he was short of fuel. He spoke in English to the formation leader, then started to elaborate to me in French. As a consequence, the formation's radio discipline began to turn pear-shaped and we achieved an Anglo/French babble that nobody could understand. Perhaps it was all too much for Colmar radar whose controller promptly announced that his radar equipment was off-line. With four jet aircraft close together, working two languages (one of which the leader did not understand), adjacent to mountains, still above cloud and with no immediate legal means of getting below the said cloud, the babble factor increased exponentially. *La polyvalence* started to assume a whole new dynamic.

Sergent-Chef Marion, who decided to remonstrate with the Colmar controller, spoke in French. The Lightning leader, Tony Alcock, decided that he, too, should take issue with the Colmar controller, only in English. All of us, however, realised quite quickly that this tactic was unlikely to be productive. The Lightning man therefore made a couple of calls to his number two (still half-a-mile behind the rest of the formation) then remembered that he had an Anglo/French facility in the form of me. Into this toxic mix, Marion persisted to warn Colmar and me in high-velocity French – with the odd bit of pidgin-English thrown in – of his ongoing fuel problem. If all of this makes little sense to the reader, be assured that at the time it made absolutely no sense whatsoever.

With the radio babble now more or less continuous, the Lightning leader struggled to get a word in edgeways, although an opportune moment arose eventually. He pressed his radio transmit button to articulate the time-honoured words: "What the .... is going on?" All of us, I'm sure, would have liked to have asked the same question but as formation leader he was supposed to know the answer. The effect on Sergent-Chef Marion was dramatic. "*Je dégage,*" he cried, which loosely translated means: "I'm out of here." As thoughts of 'shit' then 'good riddance' danced through my mind, I watched as his Mirage 3 broke away from the formation. The trouble was that Marion did not *dégage* completely. His aircraft turned away, for sure, but instead of placing himself at a safe distance he travelled about fifty yards (perhaps that should be meters – either way, it wasn't very far), stopped the turn then held a position adjacent to and slightly higher than the rest of the formation. It was as if he had experienced a sudden change of heart as he broke away.

His continued position close to the formation was hazardous but, even worse, because of his height advantage he probably couldn't see us. In all likelihood he thought he was well clear.

The scene was now set. Potential disaster loomed. Sergent-Chef Marion, apparently oblivious of our presence, turned towards the formation and descended. The underside of his Mirage 3 consequently impacted with the topside of Tony Alcock's Lightning – a bang on the canopy which immediately shattered. Tony Alcock, who abruptly found himself in 400 knots of airflow, owed his life to the scant protection provided by the Lightning's small section of forward canopy. Sergent-Chef Marion, meantime, really did *dégage* to vanish from sight towards the far horizon. Meanwhile, I was transfixed by the spectacle of a canopy-free Lightning from which various bits persisted to fly off. I prayed that one of them would not be the pilot. Perhaps the prayer was answered because, before I could say '*zut alors*', Tony Alcock and his Lightning had descended into cloud and disappeared from the scene.

One moment I'm at the centre of a four-ship frenzy, the next minute I'm on my ownsome and quietly toddling along wondering where the hell everyone else had gone. Talk about surreal. Although the most bizarre part of the whole episode was yet to happen.

Tony Alcock's Lightning now shot back up out of the cloud to resume its exact same position before he left. It was if nothing had happened, as if he had been there all the time. To say I was impressed by Tremblers' formation station-keeping would be an understatement. In truth, I suspect my eyes must have been out on stalks. I dreaded to think of the state of Tony Alcock's eyes not to mention his thoughts when he contemplated how close he had come to another mid-air collision; two in a day would have been quite tough.

I shall never forget the sight: no canopy; scarf flying in the wind; various leads, radio cables, seat strap ends flailing about. Snoopy and the Red Baron would have been mighty proud of Tony Alcock at that moment. He stared across at me. Despite his face-mask I could detect a wide-eyed, panic-stricken look.

Later, I learnt that when he had plunged into cloud he had become instantly disorientated. At a height of some 3,000 feet and knowing that the Vosges mountains were in the vicinity he had decided to go for the option of last resort – to pull his ejection seat handle. The ejection seat's delicate mechanisms, though, had just been thwacked by a twelve-ton Mirage 3.

He tugged violently at the main ejection seat handle, then the alternative handle, but it was no good: Tony Alcock's ejection seat would not function. Still in cloud and hurtling in God knows what direction he therefore hauled back the Lightning's stick. His destiny, however, must have been regarded kindly by the deity for, by apparently sheer good fortune, the Lightning was not inverted and he did not haul himself straight into the side of a mountain. When he popped back up out of the cloud to return to his original formation position as if by magic, one can only wonder at the degree of disbelief, and the intense mix of anxiety and astonishment, that must have been careering through his head.

Tony Alcock, apparently, had achieved the seemingly impossible and practicalities had to be faced. The immediate priority was to get his Lightning and my Mirage 3 below cloud and in sight of Colmar airfield. I visually checked over the Lightning as best I could and noted that he did not appear to be obviously injured. His radio did not work so, by a system of pointing and hand-signals, I indicated to him to formate on my aircraft. He acknowledged with a thumbs-up sign. The cloud thinned at that point and I was lucky to glimpse the ground and to fix our position. Tony Alcock, despite his predicament, held a good steady formation station while I led him towards the runway at Colmar airfield where, at the last minute, I overshot from the approach while the Lightning landed.

With the precarious state of the Lightning's ejection seat, the jolt of landing might have caused the seat to be set off, but this did not happen. Nevertheless, Tony Alcock's egress from his Lightning cockpit at the end of his landing run was evidently at world-record speed. As for me in my Mirage 3, I did a quick visual circuit during which, from my position downwind, I held my breath as I watched him every inch of the way.

Within a short space of time, two seriously damaged aircraft were on display for everyone to inspect. The Lightning never flew again. The subsequent Board of Enquiry produced a host of sensible, if predictable, recommendations on language, discipline, organisation, and air traffic control. Tony Alcock was whisked off to hospital where he was pronounced fit apart from superficial damage to his eyes. He was given special eye drops, told to go to bed early, avoid alcohol, avoid straining his eyes in degraded light conditions, and steer clear of noisy places where people were smoking cigarettes.

That evening, at a party in the mess, which in terms of wildness must have equated to that on my arrival at Dijon, I bumped into the large frame of Tony Alcock. It was the first time I had seen him since he had been taken to hospital. The hour was late, in his hand he grasped a highly alcoholic 'Black Velvet' drink, the room was dark, the air was thick with the smoke of Galloise cigarettes and, as a final affront to the doctor's prescription, the noise levels were remarkably high. As might be expected with a group of fighter pilots after such a day, the raucous talk was rapid, the descriptions graphic, the punch-lines hilarious. Our laughter had a nervous edge, no doubt, but then we all experienced strong feelings of relief that nobody had been hurt. If conversation became hard in the boisterous atmosphere, this appeared to matter little in Tony Alcock's case: his facial expressions told their own story. Perhaps I was a little slow, but as I observed him comprehension dawned in the end. It occurred to me that his life would never be quite the same again after today. I realised, too, that he would not be alone in that respect.

Chapter 20

LAST FLIGHT
OF THE P1

*Wing Commander Graham Perry, Binbrook
Open Day 1982, the day the P1 was first
shown in its restored state.*

GRAHAM PERRY'S P1
PREDICAMENT

On the grass beside the parade
ground at RAF Henlow stood
the English Electric P1 aircraft.
Nearby was the English Electric P1A. Parked there
throughout the 1970s, these
two machines were the prototype supersonic research aero-
planes which eventually
developed into the English
Electric Lightning. The two aircraft, as the forerunners of all
Lightnings, were thus iconic.
The P1A version, designated
WG763, was owned by the
Science Museum while the P1,
designated WG760, remained the property of Her Majesty's Royal Air
Force whose senior members, at the time of this tale in 1982, were preoccupied with other issues.

144

The two machines had endured something of a love-hate relationship with Henlow's run of officer cadets. Before a passing-out parade, the young men and women were required to polish the airframes until the surfaces sparkled like magnificent mirrors. On the nights before Big Days, the officer cadets would work away, their fingers blackened by dreaded dabs of Duraglit polish and walloping wadges of Wadpol. "What's this, what's this?" the OCTU (Officer Cadet Training Unit) squadron warrant officer would cry as he inspected the cadets' handiwork: "a greasy mark?" The OCTU warrant officers were strong characters – a unique bunch. Never would I fail to recollect the occasion, marching on the parade square, when a booming voice demanded: "Keep those chests up and those chins in!" A brief but horrible hush was followed by: "BOTH chins Mr Perry!"

Like all strong characters, the OCTU warrant officers would get their way and as a result the P1 and the P1A's airframe skins, constructed of pure aluminium on top of alloy, began to disappear molecule by molecule into the dabs of Duraglit and the wadges of Wadpol. Towards the end, one of the more enterprising (and presumably the last) of the polishers applied a pot of clear polyurethane varnish to the airframe surfaces but alas, this proved ultimately in vain. The officer cadet training unit moved away from Henlow to relocate at the RAF College at Cranwell, the P1 and the P1A were abandoned, their surfaces started to corrode, past labours were neglected. The airframes began to look gradually more forlorn as the years went by, and the engineers on the station started to fret about their charges. By the early 1980s, the deterioration became so bad that clearly the two machines, if they were to survive, needed to be sent elsewhere.

The Science Museum, invited to reclaim their property, took away the P1A while the P1's future remained under discussion. The Royal Air Force at that time still had in service some seventy operational Lightnings whose only base was at RAF Binbrook in Lincolnshire. This, therefore, seemed the obvious place for the P1. To those senior minds for whom the exercise involved nothing more than issuing a directive, the move from Henlow to Binbrook suddenly became a brilliant, even urgent, plan. "That's fine with us," said Henlow to Binbrook, "but if you want it you must come and get it. Furthermore, this is to be a no-cost exercise and the Abingdon lot can't help with the move because they're busy fighting the Falklands War."

At that point, as I was the wing commander in charge of engineering at Binbrook, the problem promptly became mine. With some trepidation, I sent a small team from Binbrook led by the irrepressible Warrant Officer

Stott. The team members, having ventured the three-hour journey down the A1 road, were pleasantly surprised by what they found at Henlow. Although corrosion had just about eaten away the P1's lower wing skin aft of the left wheel well, and the main wheels were locked solid, these problems could readily be sorted out by the application of much WD-40 and the gentle attention of the engineer's good friend (a somewhat large hide-faced hammer).

Taking apart and transporting aircraft was the speciality of the RAF's 71 Maintenance Unit at Abingdon. However, we received confirmation that, thanks to Argentina's generals, the maintenance unit's help was not available. "That's just too bad," my station commander told me, "I still want that P1 here at Binbrook in time for our open day, just before I'm posted."

"Yes, sir."

"It's an engineering problem," he said.

"Yes, sir."

"It's therefore your problem," he said.

I drove down to Henlow. I found that the good warrant officer and his team had been correct, all things considered, the P1 really wasn't in too bad a condition. I discovered that the two Armstrong-Siddeley Sapphire engines could be turned by hand. Most of the instruments were in place, although the Machmeter was missing. This struck me as close to sacrilege; that key instrument – the very device that had recorded Mach 0.85 on the 4th of August 1954 when Roland Beamont had taken this revered aircraft up for its maiden flight – had gone walkabout. However the airspeed indicator and the artificial horizon were still in place. The control column was stuck fast and the throttles were stiff, but these could be fixed. My mind began to race. I thought about the tale of the wing commander engineer who, in 1968, had taken off in a Lightning by mistake. His aircraft had no canopy and his seat was an old orange box (or so the story went) but he managed to get the machine down okay. Could I possibly – perhaps – maybe consider this as some sort of precedent?

I noted that the cockpit seemed roomier than the Lightning's. It looked quite comfortable, actually; I could fit in there, no bother. I asked the Henlow folk to produce a hydraulic rig which, when applied to the relevant part of the P1, freed the control column and caused the control surfaces to move smoothly after some initial roughness. When a twenty-five kilo-volt-amp Houchin ground power set was plugged in to the P1's wheel well, the aircraft's electrics all appeared to behave as advertised. I glanced at the

English Electric P1.

hopeful faces of my Binbrook colleagues who watched me closely. I looked again along the length of P1, at the airframe sides, at the wing surfaces. Possibilities continued to rush through my mind. To hell with it, I thought, to fly the damn thing would be a lot easier than dismantling then rebuilding it.

The officers' mess at Henlow was a large building, but without the officer cadets, the whole structure had a gloomy, lifeless air, haunted by echoes of the past. The next day, though, as the early morning light filtered into my room as well as into my consciousness, I knew that this was not the reason for my restless night. However there was no time to bother about that, neither was there time for breakfast (in any case, I was too nervous to think about food). After a quick shave, I dressed hastily then went to my Land Rover parked by the mess. I drove up to the Henlow parade ground with mixed feelings. The die had been cast, I told myself, there should be no going back now. Suddenly, my heart missed a beat. Overnight, the P1 had been manhandled off the grass and on to the tarmac. The aircraft looked primed, business-like, ready to take to the air. The time for words had passed; action was needed now.

A fuel tanker, driven down from Binbrook, was alongside the P1 as AVTUR fuel was pumped into the aircraft's wing tanks. A scream emerged from the Houchin's big diesel engine. Nearby, a team of firemen stood anxiously, ready for trouble. When the fuelling had finished, I climbed the cockpit ladder to check the fuel quantity gauges. They read zero. I was tempted to tap the glass face of the gauges but remembered a previous occasion when such imprudence had resulted in my cut knuckle and a lapful of glass. Instead, I tapped the adjacent console. The gauges immediately jumped from zero to 1,000lbs but this was still insufficient for my flight. The refueller's gauge, though, testified that 4,600lbs of fuel had been delivered. I decided to believe that figure.

Willing hands now helped me to strap into the cockpit. The P1 cockpit differed considerably from the Lightning's, nonetheless with the benefit of several flights in the Lightning T5 twin-seat trainer, I found the P1 felt reasonably familiar. I sat on a Hawker Hunter combined parachute/dinghy pack, loaned by co-operative chums from RAF Brawdy. Carefully, I placed a blue cloth hat with earpads on my head, then a Mark 1 protective bone dome – dated but still effective. On my hands I wore a pair of new-ish cape leather gloves, aircrew-for-the-use-of. I re-examined the local area maps I had borrowed, also the copy of my flight plan, and the meteorological forecast for my route. I had no face mask and thus no facility to breathe oxygen or to speak on the radio, but these resources were not required: the aircraft's oxygen bottles had been removed, and the flight would be outside controlled airspace under visual flight rules and without radio, just like my Tiger Moth flying all those years ago.

I went through the cockpit pre-start checks as best as I could, then raised one finger to the start-up crewman who clutched a CO2 trolley fire extinguisher. He returned my signal. I reached for the number one engine start button and pressed it. I waited apprehensively for the 'wheee' of the starter followed by the crackling sound of the ignition system but a pregnant pause ensued, followed by...silence as the engine wound down. Nothing happened; there was no ignition. "We'll have to give it the 2B pencil treatment, sir," said one of my Binbrook fitters as she grinned at me, "a bit of graphite across the insulator should do the trick." Sure enough, this worked. My second attempt resulted in a satisfactory 'wheeee' followed by a small boom-booming sound as the engine sprang into life. I stared in amazement as the engine's RPM and temperature gauges began to wind up. I shook my head: I could barely believe what I saw. My astonishment was reinforced when the second engine's gauges indicated that it, too, had spun up and lit successfully.

I signalled for the Houchin's ground power to be disconnected and I watched with a sense of misgiving as the P1's internal electrics took the load. The voltage output was quite variable – anything between twenty and twenty-six volts – but, inconsistent or not, at least there was voltage. I focused on the hydraulic pressure. The hydraulic dolls-eyes remained black, even when I exercised the flight controls; there was nothing wrong in that department as far as I could see. I therefore reached for the lever on my right side, pressed the small switch at the top and waited for a re-action. To my relief and ongoing amazement, the hydraulically-operated canopy began to lower. Soon, with the canopy fully down, I was able to push the lever to the 'canopy locked' position.

Now ready to attempt to taxi the aircraft, I signalled for the start-up crewman and a growing crowd of onlookers to move well clear. They seemed not to need a great deal of encouragement. I therefore cautiously released the wheel brake lever, allowed the P1 to roll forward a few feet, then reapplied the brake. The P1 stopped; the brake function was satis-factory. Next, I released the brake lever slightly and this time, as the aircraft rolled forward, kicked the rudder pedals firmly left then right. When the machine followed obediently, I felt a small thrill of satisfaction: another crucial hurdle had been overcome. Just one major obstacle remained now – the take-off run itself.

The goings-on outside the cockpit suddenly assumed renewed impetus. I watched smugly as the unbelievers hastily acted to move barriers, drive parked cars to other spots, and generally tried to control the ever-swelling throng of spectators. I did a U-turn out of the parade ground, moved past St Andrew's Church, then applied full right rudder and a touch of brake as the P1 swung smoothly into Burnett Avenue. I taxied twenty yards up the road, eased into a shallow right-hand bend, then on to a nice straight section of road that must have been built, I reflected proudly, by the Ro-mans themselves. As I progressed, I noted how the admiring masses gazed and gesticulated with enthusiasm. I acknowledged with modest thumbs-up signs and just the occasional royal wave for the benefit of any children in the crowd. Before long, though, casual reverie had to be put to the back of my mind. My fullest powers of concentration would be needed shortly; I was nearly at the selected take-off point, another stretch of straight Roman road.

I checked carefully above and all around as I approached the take-off area. On the ground, obstacles had been cleared away, side roads closed

off, and parked cars removed. All looked clear. I craned my neck upwards
as I searched for signs of conflicting air traffic, but I saw none. Now I
slowed to a stop and held the P1 on its brakes. I had a final check around
the cockpit: engine revolutions and temperatures; flight instruments;
electrics; hydraulics; canopy re-checked; controls full and free movement;
maps safely stowed. Everything appeared to be in order. I was ready for
take-off.

With my eyes keenly monitoring the engine instruments I used my left
hand to ease both throttles forward. The P1 began to lean ahead like an
anxious runner ready for the off. At this juncture, however, the brakes still
held the machine in check even though the engines' revolutions increased
steadily – *4,000 RPM*...despite the soundproofing effect of my headset, I
could hear the rising roar of the Armstrong-Siddeley Sapphires...*4,500
RPM*...I noted the first signs of brake slippage but still maintained a firm
handgrip on the brake lever...*5,000 RPM*... the airframe started to shake
as the pent-up energy of the P1's engines was further released...*5,500
RPM*...the brakes were being seriously challenged now...*6,000 RPM*...the
brakes were slipping badly so I released the brake lever and...we were off!

At once, I pushed both throttles fully forward. A heightened thunder
from the two Sapphires signified the engines' potency as they thrust me
eagerly along the take-off run. I focussed my attention outside the cockpit;
trees flashed past; buildings on either side became a blur; houses at the
end of the take-off run began to loom. I glanced at the airspeed indicator:
sixty knots. The trees and buildings rushed by at an ever-increasing rate
as I held the twin throttles forward. When I checked my airspeed again –
eighty knots – I knew I was committed; there would be insufficient distance to stop safely now. I stared bleakly at the houses ahead and my inner
turmoil instinctively intensified. The next glance at my airspeed indicator
revealed 100 knots; by this stage invisible fingers were trying to tie knots
in my intestines. At 130 knots I pulled the stick back but it was no good:
I felt the tailplane hydraulic jack stall. With the windscreen now ap-
pallingly full of houses, at 150 knots I yanked back the stick once more.
This time, thank heavens, something happened and the nose-wheel lifted
off. A short pause ensued before – wonder of wonders – the main wheels
became airborne. There was little time to breathe a sigh of relief, though,
as my rate of acceleration began to increase exponentially. With my airspeed at 180 knots I pulled the stick back a bit more and then...quite suddenly...I realised that I had made it. The lack of any kind of violent

movement or crashing noise meant that I had overflown the houses, albeit by the narrowest of margins.

The P1's acceleration now had to be tamed. It was too risky, I felt, to raise the wheels after all those years so I left the undercarriage operating button well alone. Still monitoring the RPM gauges, I began to bring the throttles back and simultaneously I eased the stick forward. I aimed to level the aircraft at a height of around 2,800 feet. A glance at my flight instruments showed that the main gyro compass was not working, but fortunately the E2B standby compass seemed serviceable. I turned the P1 onto a heading of 020 degrees as I aimed for Binbrook. I juggled the twin throttles to achieve around 5,500 RPM; this equated to an airspeed of around 240 knots – plenty fast enough with the undercarriage down. A quick check of my watch showed the time to be just before 0830. Great, I thought, I'll get home before the morning rush of aircraft using the low level navigation routes and the east coast military firing ranges.

Unable to communicate with anyone, I knew that I would have to rely on my map reading and dead reckoning skills. I looked at my watch again: 0832. At an airspeed of 240 knots, the P1 was covering four nautical miles a minute. Armed with this information, my time and distance calculations would be relatively straightforward. Before long I spotted the town of Peterborough with its distinctive brick chimneys. A quick inspection of my map confirmed that I needed to turn starboard a few degrees. The aircraft felt quite jumpy in the turn, then I noticed that the 'feel' switch, on the left cockpit console, was still off. I placed the switch on and immediately noticed the improved handling characteristics. The trim switch on the stick now worked in pitch, though not in roll; overall the aircraft was far more comfortable to fly. Suddenly I realised how much I had begun to enjoy myself: the engines rumbled away as if nothing unusual had been demanded of them, the cockpit floor shook a little and I was aware that I felt cold, but so what – who cared? This was really something.

For a moment I pondered my past flying experiences. Though a professional engineer, not a pilot, I had logged a fair number of flying hours in a variety of different aircraft. The memory of my first-ever flight jumped out at me. I was just eight years of age when my father took me, in 1953, to Ramsgate airport, newly rebuilt having been bombed in the war. A small aeroplane, a Miles Messenger, could be seen as it pottered round the airfield giving joyrides. At length, with my nose pressed up against the fence by a gate – 'only passengers beyond this point' – my father took pity on me.

"You go," he said.

"Are you coming too?"

"No, it's a bit expensive – five shillings (25p). You go if you want to."

"Thanks Dad!"

A middle-aged couple came too, the man sat in the front next to the pilot, the lady and I were in the back. I had to be lifted up onto the wing root so that I could climb into the back seat. I was surprised by the noise level when the engine started, and the taxi across the grass to the take-off point was bumpier than I expected. As the Miles Messenger accelerated during the take-off run, I looked back and waved at the diminishing figure of my father. As the aircraft climbed, I could hardly believe the fascinating beauty of the ground from the air. Everything seemed so logical, so much more pronounced – the green of the countryside, the white of the sea's surf, the blues and greys of the sea itself…

The P1, rocked by an area of local turbulence, began to drift off course. I made a swift correction then noticed the line of the coast ahead. The unique shape of the Wash appeared on my starboard side but the inside of the canopy had started to mist up and views on my extreme right and left were becoming quite restricted. The visibility ahead was good, though, as I followed the coastline past Wainfleet range, the holiday resorts of Skegness and Mablethorpe; the latter town with its distinctive, if antediluvian-looking, ferris wheel and vast stretches of sandy beach. Soon, as I crossed the wide mouth of the Humber estuary, I could make out the small blob of white which marked Spurn Head's lighthouse. With such conspicuous navigational aids, I was now confident enough to put away my map. I needed to concentrate on my approach and landing at Binbrook.

As I eased the P1's control column to the left, at the same time I reduced engine power to around 4,000 RPM to bring the speed back and descend slightly. Now over my home patch, I began to recognise local features as I took up a south-westerly heading for Binbrook airfield. I flew past Patrington village then aimed for the gap between Pyewipe chimneys and Grimsby's fish dock tower. Before long, as the P1 recrossed the Humber estuary, I brought the throttles back to achieve 3,000 RPM. At this juncture, with my altitude passing 2,400 feet, I could make out Waltham windmill beyond the estuary. I noted poor visibility to the south but despite this I soon managed to spot the black asphalt of Binbrook's runway. I was nearly home and dry.

I carried out pre-landing checks as far as I could recall them, then I concentrated on the runway perspective – not too high, not too low. With flap selected down, I adjusted the engine RPM to 3,500. I began to get low on the approach so I inched the throttles forward...3,700 RPM...3,800 RPM...still not enough...3,900 RPM. Back on a reasonable-looking approach path, the runway's aspect appeared okay again. Through the haze to the south, I gained some comfort from the sight of familiar territory. On either side of the P1, my peripheral vision picked up Hatcliffe village and Croxby pond as these features went past in a blur. But now I was close to the airfield boundary; white markings on the runway surface had started to rush towards me. I had to force myself not to stare at them, not to become mesmerised like a startled rabbit. I knew I had to look ahead, to use the general picture to assess height and other criteria. That was easy to say...pilots were trained in the techniques...for me this was...new.

Immediately I felt a hefty thump as the main-wheels slammed onto the runway surface. At once, I brought the throttles back to the idle/idle position and felt for the brake lever. Without a tail parachute, my speed would be hard to control and the brakes were pretty ineffective at high ground speeds. I noticed some vehicles – tractors and fire engines – at the far end of the runway. What the hell were they doing there? Despite my high ground speed, I applied the brakes as hard as I could but it was no good...I was rushing towards the vehicles...a collision was inevitable...for heaven's sake *move out of the way you lot...*

I was suddenly aware that someone was shaking me gently by the shoulder. "Wake up," said my wife, Bobbie.

"What?"

"You're restless – all over the place."

"Oh."

"And you've been making funny noises."

"I have? Sorry."

"You must have had a nightmare."

"A nightmare?"

"Yes. A nightmare."

I sat up in bed. "My goodness," I said, "it *is* a nightmare...today's the day."

"What day?"

Patiently, I explained. I told her how, over the past couple of days, WG760 had been dismantled by our team at Henlow. By the previous evening the fuselage sections and various pieces had been secured on to

RAF Scampton's low loader lorries. Today the wings would be added to the load before the whole lot would be driven to Binbrook.

"I'm sure it'll be all right," she said.

Sure enough, the P1 arrived safely the next day. One month later, I would reflect with pride on how the old aircraft had been rebuilt and restored by Chief Technician Chapman's dedicated team in Binbrook's Aircraft Servicing Flight. WG760, the grandfather of all Lightnings – the machine which, soon after its maiden flight in 1954, had been the first British aircraft to exceed Mach 1.0 flying straight and level – would be preserved for posterity. Twenty-eight years after that first flight, the aircraft still looked perfect. The star of the static display at RAF Binbrook's 1982 open day, the P1 looked so operational with its canopy open and its safety flags revealed that one spectator even asked when it was going to fly.

A few years later, when RAF Binbrook closed, WG760 found a new home at the Royal Air Force Museum at Cosford where in 2010, another twenty-eight years on, the machine still looked as good as new.

Fancy having nightmares over a little thing like that.

Chapter 21

COMBAT CLASHES

JIM WILD'S WINNING WAYS

All may be fair in love and war although some, it seems, do not necessarily see things that way. It was in August 1980, when I was a member of 5(F) Squadron, that we were visited at our base at Binbrook, Lincolnshire by a United States Air Force specialist squadron. Our American visitors, known as the 'Aggressor Squadron', were equipped with Northrop F-5E fighters painted to look like the potential enemy of those days: Warsaw Pact aircraft. The Aggressor Squadron pilots, trained in tactics likely to be employed by the Warsaw Pact, were tasked to instruct others in the potential enemy's methods. The swing-wing Mig 23 (NATO code-named 'Flogger'), for example, could in theory fly faster and higher than the Lightning but by exploiting their weaknesses we learnt how best to gain advantage over the adversary.

The initial exercises, with one Lightning pitted against a single F-5E, refreshed our basic combat skills. After that, the sorties became steadily more interesting as we progressed to combat missions with two-versus-one and two-versus-two. It was on one of the later exercises, with two Lightnings against one F-5E, that I decided to conspire with my fellow Lightning pilot to liven up the proceedings. Having sneaked off to a secluded office, I made a clandestine telephone call to the radar unit. We pilots maintained good terms with our radar controllers and during the conversation I reckoned that I recognised this man's voice. Fortunately, he was co-operative when he heard my scheme and I could not avoid a small smile of satisfaction at the conclusion of our telephone call.

As planned, the two Lightnings took off ahead of the F-5E. We met up with a Victor tanker, filled our fuel tanks to full, then bade farewell to the tanker crew and changed radio frequency as we prepared for the interception. On instructions from the controller, I accelerated to a speed of Mach 1.3. This put me some seven miles ahead of the other Lightning. At about that stage we heard the drawl of the F-5E pilot's voice on the aircraft radio. The clipped comments in his American accent suggested that he was ready for action.

He did not, however, have to wait long. Quite quickly, as I closed up at supersonic speed from behind, I was well-placed to fire a stern-attack missile. On my call of "Fox 2" (missile fired from astern) he immediately initiated a violent evasive manoeuvre which, regrettably from his point of view, meant that he turned directly towards the other Lightning. It was not long, therefore, before my colleague also called "Fox 2".

Meanwhile, I had zoom-climbed, trading speed for height to position my Lightning well above the F-5E. My colleague did the same and soon, to the chagrin of the F-5E pilot, both Lightning pilots were able to call two more successful missile firings. By this stage we had consumed a considerable amount of fuel and needed, therefore, to return to base *post haste*.

At the subsequent debrief, the F-5E pilot complimented us on our tactics and expressed surprise about the initial engagement. He had been on the same operational frequency as us and was bewildered as to why he had not spotted us in time. I now revealed our ruse. In my pre-flight telephone conversation with the radar unit, I had arranged that the controller should add ten miles to all reported ranges, a ploy that was bound to confuse the 'enemy'. The F-5E pilot's jaw dropped when he heard this. Silence ensued for some moments until he expressed astonishment that so-called friends could stoop to such underhand methods.

"It was a training exercise," he said, "why cheat?"

"We made a point."

"A point?"

"The fellow you don't see is the one who will shoot you down. That's a lesson from the earliest days of air combat – a lesson that's as true today as ever it was."

"But you cheated!"

"We gained the upper hand."

"Only by bending the rules."

"What rules? Would the Soviets stick to any rules?"

"The rules would be different, that's for sure," sighed the American.

"There'd be no rules. Come the Big One, the day when the Soviets unleash their full might against us, they'd come in such large formations that we'd be outnumbered by – who knows? – thirty to one, forty to one?"

"That would make it even more unrealistic for your controllers to call out false ranges."

The argument swayed back and forth and we struggled to convince our American guest. "We're Lightning pilots," I said at one stage, "by definition we are therefore 'good chaps' and not accustomed to duplicity." This attempt to lighten the atmosphere, however, did not seem to go down well.

"Humph," grunted the F5-E pilot.

In the end, despite rational points on both sides of the argument, we had to agree to disagree. On one aspect, though, we all agreed: that the Aggressor Squadron's visit had been a good opportunity to set and to analyse complex situations. Consequently, our competence had improved.

HOW TO WIN A TIE FROM MESSRS MARTIN BAKER

It was about a year later, in July 1981, that this competence was tested in another way. As part of an air defence exercise, I had been briefed, together with the pilot of another Lightning, to mount a combat air patrol off the Yorkshire coastline. We flew careful lines in the sky at an altitude of 3,000 feet while we waited for signs of 'enemy' activity. Extended 'CAPs' could become quite irksome and it was all too easy for the mind to start to wander. 'Is that a whale?' one might speculate when staring at the sea's surface. 'Has the controller fallen asleep?' could be another popular thought, or even: 'I wonder what's for lunch.'

On this particular day, such musings were interrupted when the controller announced that a Victor tanker had appeared on the scene and was ready to refuel us. "You refuel first," I said to my colleague, "I'll maintain CAP until you've finished."

"Okay," he said.

His refuelling did not take long and, as my colleague returned to resume the combat air patrol, I said that I would take on fuel now. I turned away from the CAP line and applied engine power to climb up to the Victor tanker's altitude. It was during this climb that thoughts of whales, sleepy controllers or lunch promptly vanished from my head. The first sign of trouble was a cockpit warning of 'Reheat 1' – there was a fire in the number one engine reheat zone. Immediately I carried out emergency drills. During these procedures, another cockpit warning appeared, this time to announce 'Reheat 2' – now a fire in the number two engine reheat zone. My situation was not looking good. I transmitted a Mayday distress call on the radio, a call that was answered at once by the controller who said that he would alert the rescue services.

At this stage, with further dire cockpit warnings on the emergency panel, the flight controls started to freeze up. Clearly, fire had begun to burn through the aircraft control rods. Maybe I cast a last, gloomy glance at the dark sea 10,000 feet below me, I don't remember. I do recall, though, that I tugged at my seat straps to ensure that the harness was as tight as I could possibly manage, and I forced myself to adopt a good posture. I then called "ejecting" and without further ado I pulled the ejection seat handle.

I now entered a weird, other-worldly state. I was aware of a loud bang and a violent upward thrust as I was propelled away from my warm, high-tech cockpit into a vast, protean place. Without doubt, the rules were decidedly different here. I kept my eyes firmly shut, perhaps out of instinct, perhaps, too, out of awareness of possible disorientation as the seat tumbled during the early stages of ejection. When, eventually, I opened my eyes, I was surrounded by greyness. The lack of colour or noise or contrast was in itself disorientating; the utter silence that now encircled me was almost overwhelming; the recent hectic cockpit activity seemed suddenly absurd. Maybe I wondered if my earthly life had been taken from me; perhaps I reckoned to have entered some form of interim zone – a type of purgatorial holding area where, along with others who had died at the same time as me, my fate would be decided as a new world dawned.

However, although I don't recollect a great deal of detail, any disconnect between mind and body was rapidly corrected. When I noted my continued physical existence and when I comprehended that I had been falling through cloud, reality struck abruptly as I tumbled out of the cloud base. Below, I could make out the sea. A particular spot caught my attention. The water had been disturbed and I suspected that surface froth and turmoil had been created by my Lightning as the machine plummeted into the sea. A fine, formidable fighter, once the centre of attention, the focus of triumphant talk as folk marvelled at its size and power, had been despatched savagely and without dignity beneath the waves.

I gazed up at my parachute canopy. By this time the frame of the ejection seat had been discarded, and automatically separated from me and my parachute by Messrs Martin Baker's magical mechanisms. I had carried out numerous practice drills but never before had I actually dangled on the end of a parachute in a real situation. The sensation was not unpleasant. As the parachute lowered me towards the sea and as I swayed gently to and fro, I seemed to enjoy the lack of complicated machinery to manage, the absence of clamorous radio, of Rolls-Royce engines with their persistent background hum; the aura of silence was ubiquitous. I was alone with nature.

Nature, though, could treat the unwary harshly. I needed to think about, and to prepare for, a sudden sea dip. As the sea's surface loomed I made sure that my dinghy pack, which hung some distance below me, was properly secured. Just before my feet touched the water's surface I turned my harness quick release box through ninety degrees and banged it hard. The parachute canopy, suddenly released and caught by the wind, consequently began to move away. I held my breath as I was plunged into the cold water but with my lifejacket inflated I soon bobbed back up to the surface. My training paid dividends as, more or less intuitively, I went through necessary survival drills. I hauled in a shroud line to pull the dinghy pack towards me, then I tugged at the quick-inflation device. At once, a CO_2 gas bottle crashed into life to transform the pack into a one-man dinghy that would act as my fragile but vital refuge. I located and grasped two handles on the dinghy's side, hauled myself on board then hastily turned myself over to adopt a sitting position.

By now I had a taste of seawater in my mouth, my eyes were smarting from the salt-laden air, and my face felt stung by the wind. But all these hazards had to be disregarded while I focussed on the next priorities. As swiftly as possible, I ensured that the dinghy's small canvas sea anchor was deployed to keep my back to the wind. I put up the dinghy's built-in protective canopy to cover my back and head, and I blew some air into the special mouthpiece designed to inflate the dinghy floor. At this stage, as seawater began to slop around on the floor, I had to commence the laborious, relentless task of baling. Until rescue came, I was conscious that my dinghy, that trusty lifeline, needed to be nurtured with care and respect. My 'will to live', important at any time, was especially so right now.

The wait for rescue, however, could be a long one. Unlike a multi-crew aircraft where survivors could huddle together for mutual support, my fighter pilot's solitary situation would require a special approach. Denied the luxury of team effort, if I was going to survive I might have to adopt personal ruses – think of stories, perhaps, sing out loud or remember my family. I would have to guard against the sudden, irrational rages which apparently affected some people in survival situations. Why don't colleagues react more effectively? Do they not care? Just as such thoughts were beginning to enter my head, I was startled by the roar of aircraft engines. I looked up to see a fellow Lightning pilot waggle his aircraft's wings as he flew overhead. After a short interval another Lightning, whose pilot also gave a wing waggle, thundered past. With the realisation that my position was known, I promptly felt less lonely and my morale soared.

My problems, however, were not over yet. The sea was not rough that day, nevertheless the dinghy's constant movement induced a feeling of seasickness and the non-stop need to bale out surplus water became an act of torment. The monotonous, mechanical action added to an already heightened sense of bewilderment, of feeling dazed, and exhausted by the exertion. Seawater started to seep through my clothing and into my boots. My face and fingers began to feel numb. Rescue, I reckoned, could still be a while yet. Unlike the Lightning which could cover the distance in minutes, the clattering rescue helicopter would take an age. Sometimes waves would appear, apparently out of nowhere, and my spirits would rise and fall in sympathy; a heady exhilaration at the peaks followed by the depths of depression in the troughs. The sea never allowed me to be still. I glanced at my watch only to realise that a mere ten seconds had elapsed since my last time-check. I told myself to guard against over-regular clock-watching.

I wondered again about my squadron colleagues and about my rescue. Maybe there was a problem with the rescue helicopter. I had ejected at around nine in the morning and surely rescue would come well before nightfall, even so perhaps I should prepare for a long wait. I looked up at

Top: Group of 19(F) Squadron Lightning pilots, RAF Gütersloh, Germany 1968.

Above: View from a Victor tanker of 56(F) Squadron Lightning Mk 3 in-flight refuelling. The Lightning is refuelling from the tanker's left-hand hose, 1967.

Right: Clive Mitchell arriving at RAF Watisham from Akrotiri when redeploying on 21st January 1975.

Above: 19(F) Squadron Lightnings at Gütersloh, Germany, 1968.

Above right: Alan White, right, officer commanding 5 Squadron, approx 1970.

Right: Richard Pike flying a 19 Squadron Lightning Mk 2A over Germany, 1969.

Top left: XP752. It was involved in a mid-air collision in Colmar, France with a French air force Mirage aircraft on 3rd May 1971 (as detailed in chapter 19). It sustained such damage that it never flew again.

Top right: 11(F) Squadron Lightning makes an approach to landing.

Above: Officer Commanding Wing Commander Alan White with A Flight Commander Squadron Leader R L Holmes, B Flight Commander Squadron Leader J J Seavers and Senior Engineering Officer Squadron Leader R A Jones of 5 Squadron, approx 1970.

Above: John Hall (front row, second from left) and fellow pilots at RAF Brawdy, 1977.

Middle left: Lightning aircraft operating on exercise at 11(F) Squadron's dispersals at RAF Binbrook, 1975.

Below left: 63 Squadron, RAF Brawdy, August 1978. John Hall is front centre. Five of the nine other pilots also flew Lightnings. *Back row L-R:* Ben Woods, Kevin Mason (Lightnings), Keith Skinner (Lightnings), Graham Pritchard (Lightnings), Dave Stanley. *Front row L-R:* John Botham (Lightnings), John Leeming (Lightnings), John Hall, Ray Passfield, Mike Stephens. (John Leeming and Mike Stephens were tragically killed later in separate aircraft accidents.)

the sky for signs of changes in the weather pattern. If showers developed, squally winds could be expected and then the waves would become fiercer. Perhaps, if rescue was long delayed, my eyes would have to adjust to dim light as night approached. By that stage I may see colour in the stir of the sea; hundreds of varieties of greens, blues, reds, browns. There may be music in the movement of the waves, an infinite subtlety of harmony and rhythm. If the cloud cover thickened, the colours would be harder to distinguish but the music might persist.

If the showers materialised I reckoned that I should try to catch some water to supplement the meagre ration in my dinghy pack. I would have to lean back my head, let the rain splash onto my face, trickle down my throat. I may decide to abandon the baling for a moment to allow me to hold out my hands with glee. The rain's refreshing interlude, however, could be brief; a flood of frustration may aggravate a developing sense of delirium. If the music in the waves eventually turned into high-pitched voices, I would stare ahead to see who was there. Ghostly figures may come and go. Sleep would elude me, no doubt, and I would begin to feel ever-colder. The body could adapt to the cold but not the kind of numbing cold that chilled a person to the core, and forced the mind in on itself to the exclusion of all else. Eventually, my joints would start to ache, my fingers might become so stiff as to be almost useless. Irritation may smoulder inside me until, bizarrely, I might spot...what exactly? Rescue of some sort?

Suddenly my wits were alerted, jolted out of reverie by a new noise: the distant clatter of a helicopter. The noise was intermittent at first but gradually, as the welcome racket came closer, I knew that rescue was near. The feeling of elation, hard to explain, prompted a sense of emotion, a mighty flood of relief, although I knew that I should remain calm, and show professionalism. I fumbled in my survival pack for a smoke flare to help the pilot find me and to assess the local wind direction. The helicopter's clamour increased progressively and before long I caught sight of the Whirlwind as the machine headed towards my dinghy. I held the smoke flare at arm's length, tugged at the operating toggle and half-closed my eyes as a cloud of bright orange smoke erupted to drift across the sea's surface. I watched the helicopter carefully as the pilot manoeuvred to place the winchman directly above me. The winch operator then gave a thumbs up sign and lowered the winchman towards the dinghy. I held out my arms as if for divine deliverance, which of course it seemed like.

The rescue was textbook. Inside the Whirlwind cabin I grinned and gave thumbs-up signs to the crew, but conversation was precluded by the general helicopter din. I sat down and gave a grateful nod to the winchman who wrapped me in a special space-blanket. My body heat slowly returned to normal following my forty minutes or so in the dinghy (it had felt much longer). I wanted to close my eyes and I found concentration difficult; my mind seemed to drift in random directions. My thoughts went back to when I had joined the Royal Air Force in the late 1950s. Having failed pilot selection at that time, I had spent the next eight years as an instrument mechanic in the service. Then, in 1966, I was offered pilot training. My first flying tour was on Lightnings and my current posting with 5(F) Squadron, my third Lightning squadron, meant that I had accumulated nearly ten years' worth of experience on the aircraft. I had had my moments, of course, but nothing as drastic as today's events. I thought of that ultimate glimpse of phosphorescent sea turmoil as my poor, doomed aircraft sank ignominiously to the bottom.

When the Whirlwind landed me at Binbrook, my inclination was to ask for a good, stiff drink. The station medical staff, however, had other ideas. After his initial check-up, the doctor ordered me back into the helicopter to be flown down to the RAF hospital at Nocton Hall. He was concerned about the state of my spine as the Lightning's Martin Baker 4BS ejection seat, powered by cartridges soon to be superseded by a rocket-propelled system with a more progressive rate of acceleration, was inclined to cause problems. The X-ray machines at Nocton Hall, however, revealed that my back was fine. Later, the ejection seat manufacturers, who kindly presented me with Martin Baker tie number 3226, put this down to my correct posture and very tight seat straps at the moment of ejection.

For the next few days I endured mood swings. As if replicating the ups and downs I had experienced as my dinghy followed the sea swell, sometimes I would feel incredible elation, then I would suffer a couple of days of depression. The doctors assured me, though, that this was a perfectly normal reaction. Eleven days after my ejection I was allowed to return to flying.

OF LIGHTNINGS, SPITFIRES AND HURRICANES

It was about three years later, after a posting twenty or so miles south from

Binbrook to Coningsby, that I volunteered for something rather different. Based at Coningsby were the aircraft of the Battle of Britain Memorial Flight whose aircrew, apart from the commanding officer, were all volunteers. As a ground instructor on Coningsby's Tornado aircraft, I was well placed to volunteer myself. After assessment on the Flight's Chipmunk aircraft, I flew the Hurricane initially before, after a few months, I was converted to the Spitfire. I flew, too, as co-pilot on the Flight's Lancaster aircraft. Sometimes my practice flights in the Hurricane or Spitfire would take place in the early evening when the day's primary duties were over. I found it thrilling to listen to the distinctive hum of the Spitfire's Rolls-Royce Merlin engine as I gazed down from 5,000 feet at the Lincolnshire countryside that stretched sublimely into the distance, a picture of green and purple in the setting sun. As a trained fighter pilot I was used to searching the sky up and down, left and right, well behind and I could imagine myself as a 1940's pilot looking for enemy aircraft.

"Tallyho," the formation leader might have cried as the enemy was sighted. "Line astern, go."

I could visualise the earlier scenes when the Hurricane and Spitfire pilots had waited for orders to scramble. It was like holding QRA on the Lightning force, only nerves may have been tauter back then in September 1940. There might have been a fresh, intoxicating scent of harvest in the air – a bittersweet contrast to the men's current circumstances. As the pilots and ground crews had remained on standby, poised for the call to action, some may have dozed, some might have played cards, but most would have watched the clock with anxious, over-frequent glances. A deceptive aura of calm would have masked real feelings betrayed by nervous yawns, legs crossed then immediately uncrossed. A man might have stood up from time to time to pace up and down; he may have rubbed a nervous hand over his hair as he stared skywards. Others would have watched his every move.

As I flew around in my Memorial Flight Spitfire, I could not avoid a feeling of intense admiration for my predecessors. In my Lightning days great emphasis had been placed on thorough training. The Spitfire and Hurricane pilots, though, had been required to cope with drastic demands despite, in many cases, insufficient training and a woeful lack of operational experience. The odds were formidable yet the possibility of defeat did not appear to enter their heads. Years later, a Battle of Britain pilot, Geoffrey Wellum, commented that even though the enemy's size and

less reputation were daunting (*"we suddenly realised that these fellows were serious – that they really meant business"*) it never seemed to occur to him or to his colleagues that the RAF might not win the battle. The courage of crews on both sides was captured by a Heinkel pilot who reported his experience from the Luftwaffe perspective:

> A Spitfire's tracers streaked towards us. At that moment one of our Me 109 escorts appeared behind the Spitfire and we saw its rounds strike the Spitfire's tail. But the Tommy continued his attack, coming straight for us, and his rounds slashed into our Heinkel. I put my left arm across my face to protect it from Plexiglas splinters flying around the cockpit, holding the controls with my right hand. We were eye to eye with the enemy's machine guns. At the last moment the Spitfire pulled up and passed very close over the top of us, rolled on its back and went down very steeply trailing black smoke. Waggling its wings, the Me 109 swept past us. The action lasted only a few seconds but it demonstrated the determination and bravery with which the Tommies were fighting over their own country.

Palpable dangers had not diverted brave crews from their duties; plainly preoccupied, perhaps there was no time to dwell for long on dangers in the air. For many, the waiting around on the ground before a scramble had been the worst facet. Some had recalled how, as they carried out dawn pre-flight checks, they would struggle to avoid speculation on whether the ma-

Above and left: *Aircraft from the Battle of Britain Memorial Flight.*

chine would still be around by the day's end. When satisfied with their pre-flight checks, the Hurricane and Spitfire pilots would wander back to dispersal areas lethargically to await the controller's call. A feeling of dryness in the throat, a tightness in the pit of the stomach was common.

On Lightning QRA duties, often the pilots and ground crews would watch TV as scramble orders were awaited. The Battle of Britain men, however, were denied such luxury, though they might have listened to a wireless playing nostalgic melodies in the background such as *Whispering Grass, Night and Day, A Nightingale Sang in Berkeley Square* – followed, maybe, by a selection of hits sung by the haunting voice of forces' sweetheart Vera Lynn. The atmosphere – smoothed, surreal – would have transported the young men into different worlds; the ironies of war had been emphasised, no doubt, by the wireless that wooed those who were ready for vile violence against enemy hordes.

When these hordes had been picked up by Fighter Command's Chain Home system, the controller's voice would have crackled over the loudspeaker..."squadron take-off and patrol base; further instructions in the air." To the clang of the scramble bell, pilots and ground crews would have dashed to the aircraft required to be airborne within minutes. The ground crewmen, often years older than the pilots, would have helped their young protégés to strap-in before a quick tap on the shoulder and a final word of advice: "You be careful now, sir. There ain't no sense in not being careful." Although in many cases – too many – the advice might have fallen on deaf ears, the ground crewmen had been known to watch the sky with great apprehension as they waited for 'their' young pilot to return.

Once airborne, whether in a Lightning or a Hurricane or a Spitfire, the pilot would have aimed to gain as much altitude as possible in order to meet high altitude targets. In the Battle of Britain, the Luftwaffe had often formed themselves into protective circles which were hard to break. When ready, the fighter leader might have called: "echelon starboard, go," shortly followed by: "going down now!" Then the fighters, one after the other, would have peeled off to enter a power dive. In the ensuing mêlée it soon became every man for himself. An individual pilot might have aimed to get an enemy machine in his sights by 300 yards before he closed up to 200 yards to open fire with, say, a four-second burst of fire. The sky would have been a mass of separate dog-fights.

Then an odd thing might have happened. Battle of Britain fighter pilots reported how bedlam in the sky had seemed suddenly to disappear, as if by divine intervention. One minute the men had faced frantic do-or-die fights to the last, then they were surrounded by poignant silence with not an aircraft to be seen.

And there was another curious and unforeseen dynamic, as recorded by a 43(F) Squadron Hurricane pilot:

> The Heinkel's rear cockpit bore the signs of a charnel house with the gunner slumped inside it, mutilated beyond recognition. The young pilot, his fair hair streaming in the slipstream that rushed through his shattered windscreen, was bent over the controls as if urging his stricken machine to fly. Through side window panels the two other members of the crew regarded me in silent despair. I pushed back my aircraft hood and signalled them to turn towards the coast. These were no longer enemies, but airmen in distress. If only we could have borne up their doomed aircraft with our own wings. I knew I was watching the last moments of three brave men as they went down to perish in the sea. I watched the Heinkel until, unable to fly any more, it alighted awkwardly on the sea. The fuselage broke in half. One wing tipped crazily in the air then slithered below the surface. As I circled low overhead I could see the three men struggle free and begin to swim. I called base, as did others, to fix our position and ask for help. We were some twenty miles from the coast. The three Germans would be dead long before help could reach them.

This selfsame spirit of fraternity with fellow fliers was reflected after the war – sometimes many years after the war – when former foes met up. Hatred stirred by mass brainwashing during hostilities seemed to be swept away when both sides saw that their opponents were, on the whole, good types just trying to do their duty for their country. Doubtless, the hand of providence felt by all was respected by all and maybe my involvement with the Battle of Britain Memorial Flight helped me to appreciate this.

We flew at airshows, historical events and anniversaries such as the liberation of the Channel Islands. One time, following a display at the RAF Staff College, Bracknell, a Hurricane flown by me and a Spitfire were within the London air traffic zone as the formation flew back to base. At one point the controller unexpectedly asked us to maintain an easterly heading. When we queried this, we were amazed to be told that enthusiasts at Heathrow would very much like us, if possible, to overfly the airport. Naturally, we were most happy to oblige.

In September 1990, the flypast over London that marked the fiftieth anniversary of the Battle of Britain was, for me, the culmination of my time with the Battle of Britain Memorial Flight. The Flight's seven fighters, plus the lone Lancaster escorted by a Hurricane and a Spitfire which brought up the rear of the 168 aircraft flypast, were part of a nostalgic and memorable day during which all of the Flight's aircraft were pictured airborne together for the first time.

It was some time later, when I was reflecting on my good fortune at having flown the likes of the Lightning as well as Battle of Britain aircraft, that a friend asked me casually: "How come you've managed to wangle so much good flying in your air force career?"

"Must be my winning ways," I said.

"Winning ways? What winning ways?"

"The ones that won."

"I see," he said. "But there's a problem with this theory of yours."

"There is?"

"It's a question of evidence."

"The evidence is there if you look hard enough."

"Perhaps I'd better look harder in future," he said.

"Oh yes," I said.

"Oh yes," he said.

"Beat that?" I grinned.

"Nope," he sighed, "you win."

Chapter 22

NAME GAME

RICHARD PIKE HAS HIS DAY

It was breakfast time and a stony silence seemed to greet my suggestion. This struck me as unreasonable. I was, after all, just a young lad – thirteen or fourteen years of age – and I felt that my suggestion was, actually, quite a good one. The silence persisted and unwilling to be the first to break it I concentrated on my porridge. I toyed with the grey matter on my spoon; I contemplated the criticisms of the grey matter in my head. My recent school report had noted more than once *'fails to concentrate.'* Unreasonable, I thought, as quiet curses concerning certain members of school staff went through my mind. I was particularly offended by the piano teacher's comments. My efforts in the school piano competition had been less than brilliant, admittedly, but to call them disastrous was an exaggeration unworthy of the man. How very unperceptive, I thought, he obviously lacked imagination. In any case, I never did like *Alla Turca* with its ungainly fingering requirements and jerky rhythms, and still do not to this day. The fellow Mozart, when he composed the piece, must surely have been in a pretty gruesome mood.

168

I glanced at my father. He could be severe, but then he was probably entitled to be. As the head of Fighter Command in those days, sometimes his onerous responsibilities appeared to bear down on him. He could seem distant, his mind clearly preoccupied. He did not appreciate irksome intrusion on his line of thought. In particular, he appeared to dislike tricky teenage issues. That is not to say that he lacked a sense of humour, far from it.

My sister, seven years my senior, sat opposite me on that 1950s morning. Unmoved by my plight, she perched there grimly and said nothing. My other sister, even more years my senior, was away in London. My mother, the fourth person present on that day, smiled at me sweetly. She was renowned as a fine hostess, confident, charming, and competent at coping with any social situation no matter how unpalatable or unpredictable. She would do her best always to back me up, even if the struggle appeared more than usually uphill.

Both of my parents were strong characters who held strong, rational views. They embraced high standards and expected others to do the same, especially those who held senior office. Perhaps influenced by their experiences in World War Two, they differentiated between the ambition to serve and the ambition to self-serve. My father, who had commanded a night-fighter squadron in 1941, had experienced several very close shaves, including a double engine failure at night in the twin-engined Beaufighter he flew on his first wartime operational flight. Despite the problems, he shot down an enemy aircraft on that night. By the time of his last operational sortie in June 1941 he had achieved a tally of six enemy aircraft destroyed, two probables and one damaged. He did not, however, like to talk about these experiences and I could not recall a single occasion when the subject was raised. I do remember times when, later in his life, he became physically and emotionally distressed if he witnessed signs of violence. His stern characteristics, his distinguished air, his lack of pomposity suggested a man at once straightforward and complex. Sometimes I would be aware of a certain look of his – a look that I knew well; a look that gave me a sudden feeling of unease; sheer determination which revealed the sliver of ice in his heart. From my parent's perspective, the Royal Air Force, described by the Americans in World War Two as 'a house divided', was nonetheless the be-all and end-all for them. Their deep loyalty towards the service could seem almost perverse, not least when they gave the impression that anything outside the sphere of the RAF must, by definition, be a matter of minor consequence.

All of us looked up in surprise when my father broke the breakfast silence. "Not bad," he said, "that's not a bad idea, Richard. Well done."

In turn, my astonished stare moved from my father to my mother to my sister. We had tried to conjure up suggestions at my father's request. "There's a new aircraft coming into service," he had said. "It's a remarkable machine, flies fast and furious, known just as the P1 at present. We've got to invent a good name. Any ideas?"

There had been a few ideas, but it was mine – "How about calling it the Lightning?" – which had appealed to him. "Yes," he gave me a nod of approval. "I think someone else may have made a similar proposal. It's a good one and I'll put it to the committee when we meet today."

It was some dozen years later that a particular incident brought this story back into my mind. By then it was the late 1960s, my suggestion (plucked out of thin air, like all good suggestions) had been adopted, the aircraft name had become commonplace. Furthermore, in a somewhat curious twist of fate, I had ended up as an operational pilot on the Lightning. Altogether, I served with three Lightning squadrons – 56(F), 29(F) and 19(F) Squadrons – and it was a posting to the last of these that took me to Royal Air Force Gütersloh in Germany.

My flight commander at Gütersloh, Squadron Leader Robert Barcilon (with whom, incidentally, I later shared a near-death experience: when an army electrician set an automatic stapler incorrectly, a metal staple shot like a bullet through the wall, missed by inches the heads of the flight commander and myself, and crashed through a window on the far side of the operations room), had an unusual task for me one day. "Nice little jolly for you, young Dick," he said. "I want you to fly aircraft 'A' to Wattisham, refuel at Wattisham then proceed to Warton. At Warton, pick up aircraft XN 735 which has been modified from Lightning Mark 2 to Mark 2A standard. With the larger ventral fuel tank of the Mark 2A, you should be able to fly back here directly without the need to refuel en-route."

"Okay, sir," I said. "I'll work out the navigation and submit a flight plan."

"Get a move on. Warton will expect you at around midday."

So it was that a pleasurable transit flight took me across Germany, Holland, the North Sea and England to end up, as briefed, at the Suffolk airfield of Wattisham. After a quick refuel there (my RAF base before posting to Germany), I was soon off again to head for the British Aircraft Corporation's aerodrome at Warton, near Blackpool. At Warton, I taxied-in the Lightning Mark 2, shut the machine down at a spot indicated by a marshaller, and looked across to see a smartly-suited gentleman step forward to greet me. This was unexpected. I was used to no greeting at all and he appeared a most friendly fellow. He accompanied me to an office where I signed away aircraft 'A' on behalf of Her Majesty's Royal Air Force. "Now I expect you could do with a bite of lunch," he said, "but first I want to introduce you to one or two people."

I was then driven to another part of the aerodrome before I was ushered into a reception room. A number of people were in the room and I sensed a lull in conversation as I entered, such as may happen with the arrival of royalty. I was a confident young man, buoyant, brilliant (*Alla Turca* notwithstanding), on-top-of-the-world, yet there, at that moment, I felt uneasy. I realised that my flying gear, my functional size ten flying boots, my air force-issue flying suit (aircrew-for-the-use-of) must have looked out of place amongst such augustness. A strange device stuck out of my pocket, an intriguing if innocent anti-g suit connector. Everyone else was smartly dressed, elegant, clean, and business-like.

"Allow me to introduce myself," an urbane gentleman with silvery-grey hair came up to shake my hand. A company badge pinned to his jacket stated that he was a director of the British Aircraft Corporation. "If it's all right with you," he went on, "we'd very much like to use this opportunity to pick the brains of an operational Lightning pilot. We don't often get the chance to hear things, so to speak, direct from the horse's mouth."

"Marvellous," I said. "Why not?"

The session was intense, almost overwhelming. The day-to-day operations that I took for granted were, to them, part of another world – a distant one which they appeared only to half-understand. The equipment they designed and supplied was used by us but feedback was patchy, mainly limited to communication through remote engineering channels. The chance to speak directly with a fellow from the front line was a welcome opportunity.

The interrogation began. What did I think of the gunsight arrangement on the Lightning Mark 2A? I was an instrument rating examiner, so what were my views on the layout of the instrument panel? Did the new, enlarged ventral fuel tank have a significant impact on our operations in Germany? What about the modified throttle system? We discussed the case of an engineering officer who, having inadvertently selected reheat during

ground runs, unintentionally got the Lightning airborne. The crazy guy –
a Welshman, they said – managed an emergency landing so he escaped
with his life, but it was a close thing. Then there was the vexed issue of
fire in the air, an all-too-common occurrence on the Lightning fleet. Had
I personal experience of such an emergency (I had) and were the stipulated
emergency procedures satisfactory? The questions flowed thick and fast,
the time whizzed by, I even sensed that the flying suit, the boots, and even
the anti-g suit connector may have contributed to the occasion, in a *bona
fide* sense if nothing else.

At lunch, an opportunity to relate my story about how the Lightning
got its name generated a few curious looks, but everyone was very polite.
Eventually, at the end of a notably better lunch than on a normal day, I
had to prepare for the return flight to Germany. "Thank you so much for
your hospitality," I said to the director.

"Not at all. Delighted to meet you."

The staff car whisked me away towards Lightning Mark 2A XN735
which had been placed in front of hangars. As I was driven up, I could see
at once that this was no ordinary aircraft. Everything about the machine
was new, shiny. The surfaces were pristine, the paintwork immaculate. As
I performed the traditional walk-around checks, I soon realised that I was
wasting my time. It was a bit like taking delivery of a brand new Rolls-
Royce motor car (not that I have ever taken delivery of such a car). Even
the tyres gleamed. Before long, amidst cheerful banter with the attendant
ground crewman, I climbed the ladder to enter the cockpit. It was at this
point that I must, suddenly, have begun to grow up a bit. As understand-
ing struck, I could barely believe my eyes.

Workers, staff of the British Aircraft Corporation, had begun to file out
of the nearby hangars. As the numbers swelled, as hundreds upon hundreds of folk eventually stood there quietly to watch, I realised that these
were the men and women who had toiled for months to produce the machine that I was now about to fire up and fly away. I felt humbled, moved
by such a sight. These were the real McCoy, the back-room lads and lasses,
the true powers behind thrones. Somehow, at that instant and in front of
all those people, my sense of self-confidence, buoyancy, on-top-of-the-
worldliness, seemed to modify a little. Their presence produced for me a
strangely emotional sensation the memory of which can still induce a lump
in the throat, a dampness in the eye. This was their baby, not mine. I was
merely the final link in a long, complex chain.

The return flight to Germany, as predicted, happened in one hop; en-route refuelling proved unnecessary. I therefore landed XN735 at Güter-sloh as normal, after which proceedings were routine: no staff car; no directors; no profound questioning; no fancy luncheon. I signed in the new aircraft then walked upstairs to the squadron operations room.

"How did it go?" asked my flight commander.

"It went fine, sir," I said and went on to explain about the VIP reception.

"My God," he said. "Are you about to become a name-dropper?"

"Probably," I said. "Let's face it, I'm pretty good at the name game."

"What on earth do you mean?"

"Well," I said, "it's a bit of a long story but it all started at breakfast one morning. I was just a lad at the time…"

APPENDIX A

COMPILED BY GRAHAM PERRY

LIGHTNING PROTOTYPES AND VARIANTS

Type: P1 and P1A
Number built: 2
First flight of type:
4th August 1954

Engines: 2 x Armstrong
Siddeley Sapphire
Weapons: None (P1) and
2 x Aden guns (P1A)

Two prototype supersonic research aircraft, built as part of a government programme that included the Fairey Delta 2 and other aircraft for low-speed research of new wing planforms. WG760, the P1, was the first to fly, first exceeding Mach 1 one week later on 11th August 1954. It was the first British aircraft to exceed Mach 1 in level flight, and is preserved in the RAF Museum at RAF Cosford. The P1A, WG763, had a ventral fuel tank and nose-mounted guns, and was used for supersonic gun firing trials. It is preserved in the Manchester Science and Industry Museum.

Type: P1B
Number built: 23
First flight of type:
4th April 1957

Engines: 2 x Rolls-Royce Avon
RA24
Weapons: 2 x Blue Jay
missiles

Three prototypes followed by twenty pre-production aircraft. The first aircraft achieved Mach 1.13 on its maiden flight, and Mach 2 in level flight was achieved on 25th November 1958. Extensive test flying of this fleet re-solved early problems and enabled various wing, fin and ventral tank con-figurations to be tried, and weapons systems to be tested before series production of what by then was to be called the Lightning. The nose bullet accommodated the new Ferranti AI-23 'Airpass' radar, a feature of all sub-sequent Lightnings. The Blue Jay missile, a Ministry of Supply code-name, became the Firestreak in RAF service.

Type: F1   *Engines:* 2 x Rolls-Royce
Number built: 19   Avon 200R
First flight of type: *Weapons:* 2 x Firestreak
   30th October 1959   missiles, 2 x 30mm Aden
                                       cannon

Early series production aircraft were evaluated at RAF Coltishall with the Air Fighting Development Squadron (part of the Central Fighter Establish-ment) before 74 Squadron became the first to convert from Hunters in July/August 1960. The successor to the Lightning Conversion Unit and Lightning Conversion Squadron, 226 OCU at RAF Middleton St George re-ceived the F1 in July 1963, by which time the F1 had been superseded by the F1A. Until their first T4 arrived (see later), the LCU and LCS had to bor-row F1s from AFDS and the new squadrons.

Type: F1A   *Engines:* 2 x Rolls-Royce
Number built: 28   Avon 210R
First flight of type: *Weapons:* 2 x Firestreak
   16th April 1960   missiles, 2 x 30mm Aden
                                       cannon

The F1A introduced the in-flight refuelling probe and had the UHF radio fit as build standard. 56 Squadron was the first to receive the F1A in 1961, followed by 111 Squadron.

Type: F2/F2A
Number built: 44
First flight of type:
11th July 1961

Engines: 2 x Rolls-Royce
Avon 211R
Weapons: 2 x Firestreak
missiles, 2 x 30mm Aden
cannon

The F2 was delivered in 1962 to 19 and 92 Squadrons, but the type quickly became the focus for development to F2A standard, and thirty-one aircraft were returned from the squadrons to the manufacturer from 1966 to 1970 for the modification programme. Five RAF aircraft, stored from new at 33 MU Lyneham, were modified to F52 standard for the Royal Saudi Air Force in advance of their production F53s.

The F2A, with its bigger F6-style wings, larger ventral tank and arrester hook, was the F2 improved to near F6 standard. Many pilots preferred it to the F6, certainly in the RAF Germany theatre, because its retained Aden cannon (in the nose) and Firestreak pack enabled it to have an all-fuel ventral tank. With the 200 series Avon engine it had a useful endurance at low level, its main area of operations.

Type: F3
Number built: 62
First flight of type:
16th June 1962

Engines: 2 x Rolls-Royce
Avon 301R
Weapons: 2 x Red Top (or
Firestreak) missiles

The F3 was the first Lightning to be equipped with the Red Top head-on missile and the upgraded AI23B radar. The F3 had the larger squared-off fin to match the aerodynamic effect of carrying the new missile. The Aden cannon were deleted from the F3 and it carried the smaller ventral fuel tank. The bigger engines and lower weight of the F3 made it the aircraft of choice for the Lightning solo display pilots in later years, as well as for air-to-air combat exercises on the squadrons. Consequently the consumption of airframe fatigue life of the F3s had to be very carefully managed.

As an operational air defence platform, however, the deleted guns and smaller fuel capacity underlined the F3's shortcomings (compared with the F2A in RAF Germany and the new F6) and the last sixteen of the build were constructed to near-F6 standard and later modified into full F6s. One aircraft was converted to F53 standard for the Royal Saudi Air Force.

Type: T4
Number built: 22
First flight of type:
  6th May 1959

Engines: 2 x Rolls-Royce
  Avon 210R
Weapons: 2 x Firestreak
  missiles

The T4 was a two-seat side-by-side training version of the F1A. Two proto-types and twenty production T4s were built. The first prototype was lost later in 1959 when the fin failed under load during a test flight. The early T4s were used for extensive development of the type's auto-ILS system, and for radio and rain-dispersal system trials. The first was delivered to the RAF (the Lightning Conversion Squadron) in 1962, meaning that new pilots no longer had to solo in the Lightning without any dual instruction. This former practice famously caused one tyro to return to the crewroom white-faced after his first flight, sink into his chair and say quietly: "I was with it all the way until I let the brakes off."

Type: T5
Number built: 22
First flight of type:
  29th March 1962

Engines: 2 x Rolls-Royce
  Avon 301R
Weapons: 2 x Red Top (or
  Firestreak) missiles

The T5 was the two-seat training version of the F3, with the straight F3 wing and small ventral tank. One big difference from the T4 was that instructors had to fly the T5 left-handed (the throttles were on the right hand console for the starboard seat) which was a new challenge, especially when flying in formation. Although the forward fuselage of the trainers had distinctive bulges to accommodate the side-by-side crew, this cross-section gave the air-craft a superior 'area-rule' (transonic drag reduction) profile than the single-seater, and consequently the performance of 'The Tub' was even more impressive. This delighted its fortunate passengers, but frustrated some pilots who thought that their finest moments ought to be spent alone in something better-looking and slimmer.

Type: F6
Number built: 62
First flight of type:
17th April 1964

Engines: 2 x Rolls-Royce
Avon 301R
Weapons: 2 x Red Top (or
Firestreak) missiles and
30mm Aden cannon in the
forward ventral

The F6 was an improved version of the F3 with larger, and more efficient wings that offered better subsonic performance and more fuel capacity. Of the sixty-two built thirty-nine were originals, nine were converted from F3s and fifteen from the last F3s which had been built as interim F6s. The large ventral fuel tank improved endurance and, when the front tank section was substituted with a gun pack, enabled the Aden cannon to be re-introduced. The F6 was delivered to 5, 74, 11, 23 and 56 Squadrons between 1965 and 1967. The new F6 wing also had provision for the fitting of two 260 gallon over-wing tanks ('over-burgers') which were originally designed to be jettisoned, once completely empty. However, the pyrotechnic charges employed to jettison the tanks upwards duly applied an unsurprising equal and opposite impulse downwards on the wing, and this caused structural damage. The offending cartridges were therefore withdrawn and henceforth over-wing tanks, when fitted, were fixed. Because of their drag and other limitations (e.g. the dry runway crosswind limit was reduced from 25kts to 20kts) the over-wing tanks were seldom used in the F6's later years, although they were extracted from storage, made serviceable and fitted during periods of exuberance such as the Falklands War. Alas this was irrational exuberance as far as the Lightning was concerned, because its tyre pressures were too high for Ascension Island's asphalt taxiways.

Type: F52
Number built: 5

Engines: 2 x Rolls-Royce
Avon 211R
Weapons: 2 x Firestreak
missiles, 2 x 30mm Aden
cannon

The F52s were slightly modified RAF F2s, and were the first five single-seat Lightnings to be exported to Saudi Arabia.

Type: F53
Number built: 46
First flight of type:
  1st November 1966

Engines: 2 x Rolls-Royce
  Avon 302C
Weapons: Various (see below)

The F53 was the export version of the RAF's F6, with additional wing hard points for stores carriage. This flexible fit enabled ferry tanks to be fitted, Red Top or Firestreak missiles, Aden cannon, bombs or rocket launchers (under-wing), a fuselage integral 44 x 50mm rocket pack and a reconnaissance pack. A total of forty-six were built, plus one (to replace one that crashed before delivery) converted from an RAF F6. The Kuwaiti air force received twelve F53s, and the Royal Saudi Air Force received thirty-four. The latter were the mainstay of airborne Saudi air defence from the late 1960s to the mid 1980s, and the ground-attack capability of the F53 was used with great success by the Saudis in a 1969 border dispute.

Type: T54
Number built: 2

Engines: 2 x Rolls-Royce
  Avon 210R
Weapons: 2 x Firestreak
  missiles

The T54s were modified RAF T4s and were the first two-seat Lightnings to be exported to Saudi Arabia.

Type: T55
Number built: 8
First flight of type:
  3rd November 1966

Engines: 2 x Rolls-Royce
  Avon 302C
Weapons: Various (see F53)

The T55 was the export version of the two-seat T5, but unlike the RAF trainer it owed more to the F6 than to the F3. The T55 had the F53's and F6's larger cambered wing and the full F6 ventral tank, giving it a useful endurance. Moreover the wing was the F53's version with the same hard points for stores giving the aircraft the same flexible weapons fit as the single-seater.

Of the eight built, six T55s went to the Royal Saudi Air Force and two T55s went to the Kuwaiti Air Force. One Saudi aircraft crashed at Warton before delivery and was replaced with a converted RAF T5.

APPENDIX B

COMPILED BY GRAHAM PERRY

PRACTICALITIES OF OPERATING THE LIGHTNING

Throughout its in-service life, the Lightning retained the legacy of its origins as a supersonic research aircraft. Although fully developed into an effective air defence fighter, the weapons and equipment for this role (and fuel!) had to be shoe-horned into an airframe and engine configuration that had been optimised for speed, and where internal space was therefore scarce. In engineering maintenance terms this often resulted in the need to remove, for example, an engine in order to gain access to some small component that was otherwise unreachable. Thus what should have been a three-hour job could take three days. The Lightning therefore created a generation of technical tradesmen for whom the adjective 'unreachable' represented a challenge rather than a definitive statement. Equipped with double-, even seemingly treble-joints, they were often able to tackle the most difficult jobs by reaching through the smallest holes and working round several ninety degree bends, removing and replacing (complete with wire-locking) components without ever seeing them in situ. When later, an engine had to come out anyway for some other reason, their previous work could be seen at close quarters, and it was invariably of the highest quality.

The Lightning in service proved that it was not good design practice to place one hot, potentially leaky engine and systems directly over the hot jet pipe of a second, or to route hydraulic pipes containing inflammable fluid at 3,000psi alongside hot engine components. Many aircraft were lost to fires and many more had narrow escapes when subsequent evidence was found of sprayed hydraulic fluid on a hot jet pipe ('strawberry jam').

Neither, of course, was it good practice to route primary control runs through the bilges of the fuselage, where any small fire of leaked fluids was likely to occur. Many fire warnings on the Lightning were soon followed by control difficulties, as a story in this book testifies, and folklore had it that the record minimum interval between a first fire warning and the pitch controls going slack was as little as six seconds. Just enough time for a pilot to contemplate that Sir James Martin and Mr Baker, purveyors of excellent seats, were likely to figure prominently on his next Christmas card list.

Some 5,000 modifications were embodied on each Lightning F6 during its service life, and all were directed towards improving safety, reliability,

Graham Perry in front of the 'bi-plane mod'.

performance and, latterly, longevity. Very many were associated with the Fire Integrity programme, and in addition to a scheme that comprehensively sealed the upper number two engine compartment, many drains were incorporated to pipe overboard any leaked fluids. One of these, via a small aerodynamic pylon on the fuselage side just behind the starboard wing was known as the 'bi-plane mod', because up close it looked just about big enough to count as an extra wing! In the photograph (left) the 'bi-plane mod' can be seen just above the author's right shoulder. Other exceptional modifications developed for the Lightning involved wrapping all hydraulic connections with fire-proof tape, so that any spray leaks there (highly inflammable) would be turned into drip leaks (far less so). Procedures, too, evolved: eventually all hydraulic unions in hot areas were x-rayed after being tightened to ensure that the special internal seals had been squeezed into exactly the right shape. And, by 1982, no maintenance-due point would be extended (a trivial practice on most aircraft types, within reason) without an internal inspection of the engine compartments while the aircraft was restrained and run in double re-heat on the de-tuner. (The 'de-tuner' was so-called because to call it a 'silencer' would probably have infringed the Trade Descriptions Act.) Many times these inspections ended any thoughts of an extension of flying hours and the aircraft was brought smartly into the hangar for some urgent rectification.

In all, in engineering terms, operating the Lightning was a challenge. Working on it was difficult, and what was done had to be perfect because the aircraft could be very unforgiving. One wag in the hangar, reflecting on some misfortune that had just been suffered by the other Binbrook squadron, reckoned that: "if you want to own a Lightning, all you have to do is buy an acre of land in Lincolnshire and wait…"

*George Aird ejecting from his English
Electric Lightning F1 aircraft in Hatfield, Hertfordshire
13th September 1962.
(Thanks to* Daily Mirror *Reference MP_0018484.)*

APPENDIX C

Bill Wratten
I retired from the Royal Air Force in September 1997 as air officer com-
manding-in-chief RAF Strike Command in the rank of air chief marshal GBE
CB AFC. I flew Phantoms and Tornadoes after the Lightning, and also the
Spitfires and Hurricanes of the Battle of Britain Memorial Flight. In 1990 I
planned and led the flypast over Buckingham Palace of 168 aircraft in celebration of the fiftieth anniversary of the Battle of Britain. As leader I was
flying a Spitfire Mk2.

But the Lightning was always my first love.

Peter Vangucci
After receiving my 'wings' I flew the Vampire, the Meteor and then the
Hunter. I joined 74(F) Squadron at RAF Coltishall to fly the Lightning in
1962 and moved with them to RAF Leuchars in 1964, returning to
Coltishall as 1 Squadron commander at the Lightning OCU later that year.
After attending the RAF Staff College, and following a ground tour as the
Lightning tactics and trials officer, I had the good fortune to take command
of 19(F) Squadron equipped with the Mark 2A Lightning at RAF Güter-
sloh, Germany, in early 1972. I was with the squadron for just over two
years.

Clive Mitchell

I first flew with an Air Training Corps flying scholarship on the Tiger Moth and held a pilot's licence even before my driving license. A cadetship at Cranwell led to flying training on the Chipmunk, Jet Provost, Gnat and Hunter before the Lightning at RAF Leuchars and Tengah. I then became a flying instructor on the Jet Provost at Cranwell and CFS Little Rissington. I was a member of the Poachers and then led the Red Pelicans formation aerobatic teams. I enjoyed a flight commander tour on the Lightning at Akrotiri and Wattisham. My RAF flying ended as squadron commander of a Hawk squadron at Valley. After which I moved to Saudi Arabia as chief BAe Hawk instructor and finally flying the Hawk with the UAE Air Force.

Jerry Parr

Born 12th February 1949 in BMH Rinteln, Germany, the son of an RAF officer ex Battle of Britain pilot.

After school I went to RAFC Cranwell in 1967 and was commissioned in February 1970. There followed AFT at Valley, AD and GA courses at Chivenor before going to the Lightning OCU in 1972. I struggled through that course as we all did and joined 23(F) Squadron late that year and succeeded in becoming an operational pilot after some hard graft.

A second Lightning tour took me to Gütersloh and from there much to my chagrin CFS and a tour of penal servitude at Valley. Subsequently I flew the Jaguar on 14 Squadron at Brüggen then took off down the Staff College ground tour route; my last flying tour was as OC Flying at Chivenor ending in 1993.

I took voluntary redundancy in 1996 and have never looked back since.

Stephen Gyles

I joined as a direct entry pilot in August 1965. I went through the normal training; Chipmunk (South Cerney), Jet Provost (Syerston), Gnat (Valley), Hunter (Chivenor), Lightning (Coltishall).

1968 to 1971 – 11 Squadron Lightnings at RAF Leuchars.
1971 to 1972 – Lightning simulator instructor at Gütersloh.
1972 to 1974 – 19 Squadron Lightnings at Gütersloh.
1974 to 1977 – TWU Brawdy Hunter tactics instructor.
1977 to 1980 – 43 Squadron F4 at Leuchars. (Ejected on take-off on 21st

November 1977.)
1980 to 1982 – RAF Handling Squadron at Boscombe Down.
1982 to 1987 – 27 Squadron, Tornado GR1 at Marham (mud moving).
1987 – Promoted to squadron leader.
1988 to 1990 – Squadron leader operations, Marham (kept current on Tornado)
Oct 1990 Retired.

Graham Perry

I joined the engineering branch as a university cadet whilst reading aeronautics at Imperial College London. After a first tour operating tactical helicopters and a second instructing at the RAF College Cranwell, I spent four years on exchange with the US Air Force studying and lecturing on astronautics at post-graduate level. One of my students became an astronaut and flew four missions in the Space Shuttle. Back in the UK I was to enjoy two tours on the Lightning, first as senior engineering officer on 11(F) Squadron, and then later in the early 1980s commanding the engineering wing at RAF Binbrook. I left the RAF in 1983 for a second career in defence scientific work, where I could use the new skills I had acquired in America. Among the many futuristic projects in which I took part was the British contribution to Reagan's Star Wars missile defence programme.

In the RAF I flew as many different types of helicopter and aeroplane as I could. Today I fly a wooden, two-seat Jodel, built in France in 1958 when I was in the fourth form at school.

Jim Wild

I joined the RAF in 1958, but was turned down for pilot training. I served as instrument mechanic with two years in Aden, mainly on Shackleton aircraft and then Scampton on the Blue Steel missile to 1966. At Scampton I spent all my spare time flying at RAF gliding club, dreaming of being a pilot!

Eventually, I convinced the authorities I could make it, I was commissioned, and then commenced flying training to 1970. I joined my first Squadron this year, 11 Squadron Lightnings at Leuchars then spent a further tour when the squadron moved to Binbrook. Highlights there were QRA intercepts of Russian incursions of UK airspace.

Posted then to 92 Squadron, Gütersloh, there was very exciting low-level flying policing the border mid-1970s at the height of the Cold War.

Then I went on a staff tour at HQ 11 Group, Bentley Priory.

After this, I returned to flying duties with 5 Squadron Lightnings at Binbrook (the first two parts of chapter 21). A tour as instructor on the Lightning Training Flight after my time at 5 Squadron was followed by a tour at Coningsby on ground instructional duties on the Tornado ADV, which I flew. This is the tour where I joined the BBMF (third part of chapter 21).

I finished my thirty-five years in the RAF with a tour at Finningley flying the Dominie navigation trainer, retiring in 1993.

Richard Pike

After Lightning aircraft conversion at RAF Coltishall in 1965, I was posted to RAF Wattisham in Suffolk to join 56(F) Squadron. In 1967 I moved to 29(F) Squadron, also at RAF Wattisham, and the following year I was posted to RAF Gütersloh where I was the squadron instrument flying examiner. My last Lightning flight was in April 1970, by then I had accrued just over 1,000 Lightning flying hours, and was followed by a ground tour before I was posted to 43(F) Squadron to fly the F4 Phantom.

INDEX

187